The Great Jesus Debates

THE GREAT
JESUS
DEBATES

4 Early Church Battles about the Person and Work of Jesus

DOUGLAS W. JOHNSON

CONCORDIA PUBLISHING HOUSE · SAINT LOUIS

To my parents,
Walter and Olga Johnson,
and to my wife, Ann

Published by Concordia Publishing House
3558 S. Jefferson Avenue
St. Louis, MO 63118-3968
1-800-325-3040 • www.cph.org

Copyright © 2005 Douglas W. Johnson

Scripture quotations are from The Holy Bible, English Standard Version, copyright © 2001 by Crossway Bibles, a division of Good News Publishers. Used by permission. All rights reserved.

Manufactured in the United States of America

Library of Congress Cataloging-in-Publication Data

Johnson, Douglas W., 1935-
The great Jesus debates : four early church battles about the person and work
   of Jesus / Douglas W. Johnson.
      p. cm.
   ISBN 0-7586-0862-4
      1. Jesus Christ--History of doctrines. 2. Church history--Primitive and
      early church, ca. 30-600. I. Title.
BT198.J6345 2006
232.09'015--dc22

                                                      2005032684

1 2 3 4 5 6 7 8 9 10   14 13 12 11 10 09 08 07 06 05

Contents

Abbreviations

ANF   *The Ante-Nicene Fathers.* Edited by Alexander Roberts and James Donaldson. 1885–1887. 10 vols. Repr. Peabody, Mass.: Hendrickson, 1994.

LCC   *The Library of Christian Classics.* Vol. 6, *Augustine: Earlier Writings, Selected and Translated with Introductions by John H. S. Burleigh.* Philadelphia: The Westminster Press, 1953.

LW   Luther, Martin. *Luther's Works.* American Edition. General editors Jaroslav Pelikan and Helmut T. Lehmann. 56 vols. St. Louis: Concordia, and Philadelphia: Muhlenberg and Fortress, 1955–1986.

NPNF[1]   *The Nicene and Post-Nicene Fathers.* Series 1. Edited by Philip Schaff. 14 vols. Repr., Peabody, Mass.: Hendrickson, 1994.

NPNF[2]   *The Nicene and Post-Nicene Fathers.* Series 2. Edited by Philip Schaff and Henry Wace. 14 vols. Repr., Peabody, Mass.: Hendrickson, 1994.

Preface

The origins of this book—the reasons for its existence—can be illustrated through a couple of anecdotes. First, some years ago, while I was teaching a college religion class, our admissions officer showed up with a young woman in tow who was interested in religion courses. Because I was ever eager to find new recruits for our department, I told the class to take five and turned my attention to her. I asked what types of subjects she was interested in and she said she wanted Bible courses. I assured her that we had a number of them. Then, always eager to sell my own wares, I told her that we offered church history courses as well. She gave me a strange look and asked, "Why in the world should I ever study anything like *that*?" I did my best to explain that we understand ourselves, our world, and our faith in ways that have been handed down to us. These beliefs become so much a part of us that they influence us in ways we do not know. Our views of everything are, to some extent, shaped by the traditions that have been handed down to us. I finished by suggesting that none of us reads the Scriptures "pure," but we see them through the lenses of our backgrounds. She looked me straight in the eye and said, "I read them pure." Then she walked out the door. I never saw her again.

Second, my wife and I recently attended Christmas programs at a variety of churches. One event, at a Baptist megachurch, could only be called an extravaganza. The first part was strictly showbiz, including Santa, Rudolph, Elvis, and a large supporting cast. The second part was a rather well-done portrayal of the events of the nativity. Although this second part seemed to stand well enough on its own, a third part was evidently considered necessary. Here the pastor explained the meaning of Christmas: It all had to do with Jesus coming to die on the cross to pay for our sins. Once we accepted this, and thus were "born-again," we could rest secure that our salvation was assured.

Our next visit was to a "singing Christmas tree" at a large Presbyterian church. It was a delightful program. Again, a follow-up sermonette was thought to be necessary to clarify the significance of Christmas. A sincere layman related how he was unsure of his destiny until he was told that Jesus' death on the cross took away his guilt.

Third, we attended a children's Christmas program at a Lutheran church. It had the usual manger, Wise Men, and traditional biblical characters represented. It was a pleasant experience. At its conclusion we were told that Jesus was born for one reason: so He could die and take away our sins.

Nobody should doubt that Jesus' death on the cross has been of crucial importance to Christians throughout the history of Christianity. It remains so today. The account of His crucifixion certainly can be found in the Scriptures. But surely a sufficient account of the person and work of Jesus Christ will need to relate the cross to the fullness of His ministry, including His incarnation, teachings, healing, and, of course, His victory over sin and death confirmed in the resurrection. Perhaps such a presentation also will deal more fully with the life and struggles of the believer on his or her earthly pilgrimage.

A study of the beliefs of the early Christians, those standing closest to Jesus and His times, reveals there are a number of such views of what Jesus was all about, most of which take into account precisely this fullness of His ministry. The collective views of the

Early Church about Jesus, His person and work, form a rich tapestry with many threads. Some of the Early Church fathers tried to interweave all these threads. A few stressed one or two to the exclusion of the rest. Others clung to parts of the tapestry in ways that seemed to deny its essence or its wholeness. In the course of the debates about Jesus, some threads eventually were rejected either as denying God's grace or as holding it in ways that undercut the very grace they were attempting to proclaim.

What the Church eventually came to affirm about Jesus and His work was also closely related to what is given to, and expected of, the Christian in his or her daily life. Learning what the Early Church said about Jesus gives insight into how we can cope with our present-day struggles. A knowledge of the debates in the Early Church, and how the arguments eventually were resolved, can supply us with a fuller and a richer understanding of why the Church today holds to some of its core beliefs and how the struggles of the Early Church can assist us as we attempt to come to grips with parallel questions in our own day.

We moderns—especially us in the United States—tend to subject ourselves to a kind of collective amnesia in which we cut ourselves off from our past. We orient ourselves to the future and its promises. This attitude has aided us in producing a more prosperous world with tremendous technology and medical discoveries. But because we have neglected our own past, as if under the influence of a kind of cultural amnesia or dementia, we do not fully know who we are because we have lost the memory of those experiences that in fact have shaped us.

There is actually a "history" to our disregard of history, especially when it concerns the Christian community and its faith. Some Protestant groups during the Reformation and after were rightly offended by the corruption they found in the church of their day. This dissatisfaction led to the conclusion that almost everything in the centuries preceding them was itself corrupt and should be avoided at best and condemned at worst. Somewhat later, we come to that period usually referred to as the Enlightenment. The Western world was excited by the discovery of the powers and uses of reason. A rational God, they were convinced, created a rational world, which could be understood by rational humans. Anything that did not conform to this view of the universe was to be rejected outright. Clearly, one of those things that must be cast out was religion, at least in many of its traditional forms. For many Enlightenment thinkers, the whole sweep of Christian history was irrational and therefore merely "superstition." It needed to be thrown into the trash as an impediment to progress and right thinking.

With these attitudes influencing us, coupled with our desire to be forward looking, it is no wonder that many Christians are interested in the Bible and current events, with nothing in between. This bias against the study of history and the ethical, religious, and other constraints and consequences of such study is particularly insidious when it pervades the Christian community. Christianity has a long history in which the Church has tried to work out and proclaim its basic message while simultaneously attempting to come to grips with this or that culture, philosophy, and historical setting. The faith delivered to us today is in large part the result of these struggles. In fact, during the first five centuries of the Church's existence most of the basic issues of doctrine were hammered out. Four great debates stand out as crucially important: (1) the Gnostic Controversy, in which Christianity affirmed that the Savior is the Creator; (2) the Arian Controversy, in which the doctrine of the Trinity was developed; (3) the Christological Controversy, in which the beliefs about the person of Jesus Christ were debated; and (4) the Pelagian Controversy, in which the arguments centered around issues of grace and free will. To be ignorant of these debates is to be ignorant of how we Christians came to be who we are. To know about them is to have a fuller understanding of our faith and what it means for our lives today.

Some people will never be interested in delving into such things, but those who are so inclined may well find this little book to be helpful and informative. It is intended for the many readers who are not, or not yet, professional church workers (those who are embarking on the path to become theologians or church historians); clergy and others who can use a review; and those who will never become church professionals but are interested in learning about the early centuries of the Christian Church. I hope all these individuals, and others, can gain something useful from reading this book.

In light of the intended readership of this book, I have attempted to keep matters as simple as possible. Many persons and events have gone unmentioned, though they may be important in their own right. Some scholars may object that I have included the wrong individuals and excluded the most relevant ones. It is a judgment call. I have also attempted to avoid excessive citations. When possible, references to *The Ante-Nicene Fathers* and *The Nicene and Post-Nicene Fathers* have been provided as a modern source for those who want to use this book for further study and research. These volumes are readily available at libraries and online. I have also referred to primary sources; other references are made either when an important issue is in question or when someone's comments seemed either significant or particularly interesting.

It has been said that history is written by the winners. This remark holds true for the present volume. The main characters treated will be primarily those whose ideas and beliefs emerged victorious in the theological battles. This is not a problem for this book because its main intention is to reveal how we ended up where we are. By definition it is the "winners" who have most shaped the present understanding of the Christian faith and who are thus precisely the ones on whom we should concentrate our attention. Yet almost all parties to these arguments, whatever side they took, were sincere and considered themselves to be dedicated followers of their Lord. It is hard to find the "good guys" and the "bad guys" in these controversies. The losers, too, will have their positions treated as fairly and as honestly as possible. In all honesty I like these individuals—especially the winners, the ones eventually judged most true to the faith. I believe they have a good deal to say to us today, even centuries later. We cannot, indeed, simply swallow everything they say, but I, for one, am sympathetic to them, as will probably become clear as you read this book.

The debates within early Christianity are subtle yet hideously complex. It is hoped that by stripping them to their basic concerns we will be able to see in them important statements about God, the human condition, and questions of the Christian life and salvation with which we still struggle.

Thanks are due to all those persons who have helped me in this enterprise. First, to my teachers and professors over the years, whose patience with me has bordered on the saintly, perhaps even the angelic. I am particularly thankful for the guidance of Herb Richardson at Harvard and Albert Outler at Southern Methodist University. I am also grateful to Prof. David Whitford and to Dr. Andrew Forbat for their helpful suggestions and corrections. The usual caveat is in order: The mistakes are my own. On a more personal level, I owe my wife, Ann, and my children, Cherie and Gregory, my undying gratitude and affection for their patience, understanding, and support.

INTRODUCTION

The Background
for the Debates

W ho is this Jesus in whom the Christian Church professes faith? What has He accomplished? What is His relation to God the Father? What is the human problem related to this Jesus? What is necessary for our salvation? These and similar questions—questions that grew from the Holy Scriptures and Christian experience—bedeviled the early Christians and led to the great controversies in which the core beliefs of the Christian Church and its self-understanding were hammered out.

When we approach the study of the earliest centuries of the Christian community and its beliefs, we are immediately confronted with variety, confusion, and even chaos. This can boggle the mind and fill us with trepidation about even beginning such a journey. Characters come on and off stage with dizzying rapidity, as do doctrines of every sort. Controversies pop up at unexpected times and in unexpected ways. Politics, personalities, and theology impact one another in complex relationships. Time after time, individuals with sincere, strongly held beliefs confront others who are equally convinced of their positions. At times, differing understandings of the same words lead to conflict where there need be none. On still other occasions, seeming agreement amounts to a papering over of real conflict because the same term is understood in two very different ways. In addition, the issues debated in the Early Church seem to many moderns to be rarified and subtle, with little relation to our own lives. Thus we have trouble understanding the fervor with which early Christians held their positions and insulted their adversaries as they debated the inner relations of the Trinity, the relation of the natures in Jesus Christ, and the image of God and whether we have retained it. It seems to be akin to asking how many angels can dance on the head of a pin. All these apparent roadblocks might well deter the stoutest of souls from setting out on such a study.

Despite this complexity, confusion, and subtlety, there was a unity to what was happening in the Early Church. And these debates did possess meaning that can be relevant to Christian self-understanding, even today. At their heart all the debates were really about salvation. There are two "red threads" that run through all the controversies and are intimately connected with that topic of salvation. The first concerns Jesus Christ, specifically, who He is and what He has done for humanity. The second is about the grace of God and what that means for us, specifically, what that means for our forgiveness and our reconciliation with God. These are two sides to the same coin.

Jesus Christ

It might appear so self-evident that Christians should put Jesus Christ at the center of their belief system that it does not need to be mentioned. It might also seem obvious that from the very first, believers would agree on who Jesus Christ is and what He has accomplished on their behalf. Unfortunately, the matter is more complicated. Even in the New Testament we see a variety of approaches to these issues. These approaches are for the most part complementary to one another, but nevertheless we can feel certain tensions among them.

There is no question that the New Testament writers saw Jesus as utterly unique and of central importance in their lives and in the life of faith. One of the earliest confessions of faith was "Jesus is Lord." Other titles were given to Him in Scripture as well, for example, "Messiah" (or its Greek equivalent, "Christ"), which is found throughout the Bible. Many Jews of Jesus' day desired and expected the coming of God's Anointed One, His Messiah, whom they believed would overthrow the hated Roman rulers. But if Jesus was the Messiah, He was a different kind of Messiah. Instead of defeating the Romans, He was crucified by them. For some of His Jewish followers, this likely meant a loss of faith. But for those who remained loyal to Jesus, His death on the cross was intimately tied up with God's salvation plan, which came to light in His resurrection.

A number of other biblical titles given to Jesus portray a special relationship to His heavenly Father and, at the same time, Jesus' relationship with us, His fellow human beings. For the Gospel of John, Jesus was the Word that was with God before the beginning of the world and through whom all things were made (John 1:1). At the same time John recorded that Jesus was the Word made flesh (John 1:14). For the apostle Paul, Jesus was the Son of God according to the power of His resurrection and the son of David according to the flesh (Romans 1:1–5). He is also the "second Adam," who is from heaven, unlike the first Adam, who is from earth (1 Corinthians 15:21–22). This second Adam came as God's gift of righteousness, withstood all temptation in constant obedience as the form of God in the form of a slave (Philippians 2:5–11), and died for us, for which He is glorified. He received into Himself God's judgment against Adam and us all and rose also for us as the seal of our own resurrection unto eternal life (Romans 8:19f.; 1 Corinthians 15:20, 23). The author of Hebrews tells us that Jesus is the perfect high priest because He is sent by God, but taken from among men (Hebrews 4:14–16).

Evidently a few of Jesus' early followers embraced Him as a great teacher and even as God's Messiah, but as only a man. This group may have given rise to what was later known as the Ebionites. But these folk were always a tiny minority. In fact, from the earliest times, Christians of all kinds, whatever else they disagreed about, consistently referred to Jesus in terms that were otherwise used to refer only to God. This manner of devotion to Jesus originally occurred in precisely that Jesus community where a strict monotheism was fiercely defended. As we shall see, the early questions raised about Jesus were not about His divinity, but centered almost entirely on His humanity.[1]

The Gospel writers saw Jesus as the one who came, taught, comforted, admonished, healed both body and soul, cast out demons, and was finally crucified and killed. However, this was not the end because Jesus rose again on the third day. None of the Gospel writers, of course, was writing a mere biography. Each inspired writer presents Jesus to us as a way of witnessing to some important aspect of His person and His ministry.

The precise meaning of all the titles and descriptions of Jesus falls within the province of New Testament scholarship. But taken together, all the biblical information about Jesus expresses the belief that there is something extraordinary about this man, and every biblical writer reveals Jesus in light of the resurrection. The viewpoints offered by the biblical writers leave tantalizing hints about how the multiple aspects of Jesus' ministry fit together and what they mean for us Christians today. It was the task of the early Christian leaders, thinkers, and writers to proclaim these pieces as being part of a meaningful whole. That some among them came up with differing answers form the central points of tension that served to define the debates that rocked the Early Church for hundreds of years. But whatever the particular issue, the underlying concern was for our salvation and how that is tied up with Jesus and who He was and what He did.

Grace

The second red thread that runs throughout this period of intense controversy in the Early Christian Church is grace (*charis* in Greek, *gratia* in Latin). The primary meaning of the word *grace* is "unmerited favor." Sometimes the emphasis is on one person's positive, approving attitude toward another. For example, we are told that as Jesus grew up, He progressed in knowledge and stature and in human and divine favor, or grace (Luke 2:40, 52). The early Christians had the goodwill (*charis*) of all the people (Acts 2:47). When God is the subject of grace, it refers to His positive attitude of acceptance toward a person, as when Mary "found favor with God" (Luke 1:30). Another aspect of grace is expressed especially in the writings of the apostle Paul: Grace is a free gift, given by God and unmerited by us. God accepts the unacceptable, forgives the unforgivable, and loves the unlovable (Acts 15:11; Romans 3:24; 5:15–21; 11:6; 2 Corinthians 8:9; Galatians 2:21, 3:18; Ephesians 2:8–9, and elsewhere).

God acts in history to realize His gracious will. Thus grace is found in the Hebrew Bible, the Old Testament. Two of the innumerable examples of God's Old Testament exercise of grace will have to suffice. God chose Abraham, whose reaction was to believe God despite all odds. This faith was "counted to him as righteousness" (Romans 4:3). Centuries later, God freed the Israelites, who were slaves in Egypt, and brought them into the Promised Land, despite their rebelliousness. In fact, the entire Old Testament is the story of how God in His grace watched over His chosen people with His covenant love. In the New Testament writings, grace is intimately connected with the person and work of Jesus Christ. For John, the Word that was made flesh was "full of grace and truth" (John 1:14). The word *grace* is used repeatedly in the Gospel of Luke and the Book of Acts, as various references given in this section indicate. Even where the specific word is missing, the basic meaning and intention of grace as a divine intent, motivation, or idea is often present.

It is with the apostle Paul that grace most clearly takes center stage. The word appears frequently in his writings and the concept is found everywhere. For Paul it is the aspect of grace as free gift that dominates. A devoted Pharisee in his former life, Paul had relied on a scrupulous adherence to the Jewish moral and ceremonial laws to assure a favorable relationship with God (Galatians 1:11–24). But after being grasped by the good news of Jesus Christ, indeed by Christ's appearance on the Damascus road and by His healing words of Gospel spoken through Ananias (Acts 9:1–20), Paul gloried in God's gracious acceptance of him and in God's free gift of salvation, something he could never have earned.

Paul sums up his views on grace clearly in his Epistle to the Romans. In Romans 3, Paul states that the Law is good, but it does not avail for salvation because we cannot keep it. The Law cannot make us righteous before God because, though it gives us knowledge of our sin, the Law does not lift a finger to help us. But now, Paul continues, the righteousness of God has been revealed apart from the Law:

> But now the righteousness of God has been manifested apart from the law, although the Law and the Prophets bear witness to it—the righteousness of God through faith in Jesus Christ for all who believe. For there is no distinction: for all have sinned and fall short of the glory of God, and are justified by His grace as a gift, through the redemption that is in Christ Jesus, whom God put forward as a propitiation by His blood, to be received by faith. (Romans 3:21–25a)

A little later, Paul repeats that Christians "hold that one is justified by faith apart from works of the law" (Romans 3:28). This same theme is echoed repeatedly in Paul's Epistle to the Galatians. In his Epistle to the Ephesians, Paul declares: "For by grace you have been saved through faith. And this is not your own doing; it is the gift of God, not a result of works, so that no one may boast" (Ephesians 2:8–9).

These extremely strong affirmations of God's grace have had tremendous influence throughout the history of the Christian Church. Yet in his championing of grace, Paul leaves us with inquiries that are just as tantalizing as the questions that concern the person and work of Christ. For example, when God justifies individuals, does He simply declare them righteous though they are still sinners? Or does God in some way make them actually, that is, empirically, righteous? Or is it perhaps both understandings of righteousness? Again, in what sense are we freed from the Law, and from which law are we freed? Are we only set free from the ceremonial laws, or are we also free from the moral law? These and related questions have been debated with vigor and often with acrimony within the Christian community from the earliest days until now. But the main thrust of Paul's belief and teaching is clear: Our salvation depends first and only on God's gracious working of faith in our lives and not on our own pious accomplishments. This grace is to be received by faith, which trusts in Jesus Christ, not in ourselves.

This doctrine, or teaching, concerning grace stands at the core of the Christian Gospel. It was also central to the beliefs of the early Christians: Salvation comes by the grace of God through faith in Jesus Christ. This brings us to the central theme of this book: *Salvation by grace through faith in Jesus Christ is at the heart of all the great controversies that shook the Early Church as it tried to work out its own self-understanding.* In some cases, such as Augustine's debates with the Pelagians, this is obvious. But sometimes arguments arose because a particular view of grace seemed to deny some other basic doctrine of Christianity. At other times grace itself appeared to be denied. But even where the observed disagreement was about something such as God's perfection or the humanity of Jesus, it is God's grace in Jesus Christ that is at stake.

It must be admitted from the outset that not all scholars recognize this central theme of salvation by grace. In fact, such a position has been held up to criticism and outright denial at an increasing pace for at least the last century. A primary reason for the rejection of this red thread of grace is, as we shall see, that there existed a noticeable diversity of views in the Early Church. Thus it is difficult to decide from a human standpoint which one or ones can claim the title of "Christian." As more and more literature from the period is discovered and interpreted, scholars continue to be confronted with a broad spectrum of beliefs, all of which claim to be related to Jesus and His disciples. Because of this, a tendency has developed among scholars to believe that there is no such thing as a central theme, or "red thread," that runs through the early Christian movement and its literature. Even grace itself could—and did—have a multitude of differing and often competing interpretations.

We know that a considerable body of literature reflects a spectrum of beliefs in various communities that claimed relation to Jesus and His disciples. Because the use of what the Church has come to call "Holy Scripture" excludes other documents in this larger body of literature, some scholars have questioned the process and the end result of the Bible as a basis for making an "orthodox" proclamation of a central theme in the Christian faith. Throughout the centuries, individuals have asked why some of these early documents should be included in the canon (or accepted books) of the Bible and not others. We now know, for example, that there were other documents written in the first decades of the Christian movement that claimed to be "gospels" but that have not been included in the New Testament canon. There also existed a host of other documents that some scholars believe to be likely candidates for inclusion in the canon, given the choices at the time. Had that been the case, not only would our

Scriptures be different than they are now, but the doctrines contained in the Bible also would differ from those we proclaim today. The result of potential doctrinal differences prompts scholars to compare the possible scenarios created by those differences with perceived needs of the present age. They also compare the acts of those in authority now with those in authority in ancient times, noting the way in which human ideas and power relationships affect various outcomes today and suggesting how that could have been so then. This critical self-reflection is intended to yield benefits for both church and world.

If, for the sake of argument, we suggest that all early views of Jesus and of grace were created equal and had equal rights to be considered as *the* faith, then why did one set of beliefs emerge victorious? If history is written by the victors, who are they and how did they win? Various positions exist regarding the "equality" of some possibilities. In the Church there existed groups consisting of Aramaic or Palestinian Jews with ties to the Holy Land and its long history; Greek-speaking Jews that permeated the Roman world due to Julius Caesar's grant of special privileges and former Hellenistic pagans. We shall consider these groups below in greater detail. Scholars have sought to understand how these groups, their leaders, and their interaction helped shape Christian doctrine. Some have examined the motives and methods of the "winners." Such an approach is legitimate to the extent that we already have evidence of human failings in the Scriptures themselves. Greek-speaking Jewish Christians and their Aramaic brethren had their squabbles (Acts 6:1). Paul reveals the conflict between him and Peter in Galatians 2:11–21. Other examples of human failings in the Church abound in Acts and the Gospels, the most notable being the denial of Christ by Peter (Matthew 26:69–75 and its parallels). Yet the Gospel overcomes such failings based on God's own promises (John 16:33; Romans 12:21; 1 John 5:4). A study of the methods and motives of leaders and groups in the Church must also take into account this biblical motif and revealed truth of divine victory in the end times that itself provides comfort to the martyrs and hope for the Church in all ages.

When considering the human failings of the Church fathers, one might also need to consider the human failings that can enter into the expression of belief both then and now. In the Early Church there existed a great variety of beliefs, many of which contradicted each other, yet all claiming an authority stemming from Jesus Christ Himself. Such a situation appears to exist already at Paul's time (1 Corinthians 1:10–31). The process of the selection of books to be included in the scriptural canon, or universally acceptable books of the Bible, was also far from tidy. The outcome could have been different. It must also be admitted that the shapers of Christian beliefs in postapostolic times, though saintly, were sometimes less than pious in their methods. Peter was not the last churchman to be taken back to school by a Paul. At some point, we must question whether the history of the Church is just a human history of the Fathers and their varied degrees of success or if that history is the result of God's active will seeking our salvation despite both our sin and theirs.

However many missteps there were, things did turn out in a particular way. As we shall see, there was a sifting process that winnowed out a host of varying false opinions about Jesus Christ and the Christian faith, along with the literature associated with these views. It is a reasonable position to take—and one this present book will endeavor to show to be reasonable—that this winnowing was done on the basis of salvation by grace in Jesus Christ. Even when the Fathers of the Church were less than admirable in their methods, the position they were defending was exactly that grace as they understood it.

The Holy Spirit

When we treat grace in its relation to Jesus Christ, it is important that we do not neglect the accounts of the Holy Spirit in the New Testament writings and in the Church fathers. The references to the Holy Spirit are found almost everywhere: Luke 1:35 tells us that the "Holy Spirit will come upon [Mary], and the power of the Most High will overshadow [her]"; Jesus will baptize with the Spirit (Luke 3:22); and as He comes up from the water after His Baptism, the Spirit descends upon Jesus (Matthew 3:11). Jesus is led by the same Spirit into the wilderness (Matthew 4:1); He tells His critics that it is by the Spirit of God that He casts out demons, so the kingdom of God is upon them (Matthew 12:28).

The Holy Spirit also is given to believers. In the account of the first Pentecost, the Holy Spirit is central to the founding of the Church (Acts 2). Those baptized at that time and throughout the Book of Acts receive the Holy Spirit. Paul tells us about the gifts (*charismata*) of the Spirit (1 Corinthians 12). In Romans Paul assures us that in our suffering we need not lose hope because "God's love has been poured into our hearts through the Holy Spirit who has been given to us" (Romans 5:5). Paul also tells us that this same Spirit helps us in our weakness (Romans 8:26).

Just as the grace of God is intimately connected with Jesus, it is also clear that the Holy Spirit is also involved with Jesus in human salvation. The Early Church had the task of working out just what that implies.

Jesus Christ, grace, the Holy Spirit—all are manifestly important to a Christian understanding of life and salvation. Yet as we have seen, a number of issues concerning the Christian faith are unresolved and left hanging at the very beginning of the Church. Which of the differing pictures of Jesus, if any, should be normative? What is Jesus' relation to the Father and to human beings? Which of Jesus' deeds is central to salvation: His becoming flesh (the incarnation), His teaching, His crucifixion, His resurrection, all of the above? When Paul writes that God justifies us, is this merely a declared righteousness or a real righteousness or is it both? When Paul states that we are free from the Law, what exactly does he mean? God gives the Holy Spirit. But in practice what does this mean for believers?

These are the kinds of questions that bedeviled early Christian thinkers. We might forgive them if their answers sometimes seem confused and often resulted in controversy. The earliest believers were flush with the Good News of Jesus and His salvation and were passionately desirous of working out what this meant for themselves and their Church. Some of their attempts at understanding and explaining this Good News failed. Some have been accepted as the basic teachings of the Christian community.

Both the ferocity of the debates and the subtlety of the arguments can be explained by the fact that these men understood something we often forget in our attempts to be open-minded: Ideas have consequences. Beliefs have real and practical effects upon our lives. The Early Church fathers also were aware that when we take the wrong fork in the road—intellectually as well as geographically—we can travel for some distance and remain close to the other path. However, we usually end up a long way from where we wanted to be. The Early Church fathers wanted to get the starting points of the Christian faith—the basics—as right as they could, especially because the Early Church had a strong expectation of the Lord's return as Judge of the world. That expectation matured into the understanding that the end of the world is as near as the end of one's earthly life.

Christianity and Culture

As the early Christian thinkers struggled to come to grips with this collection of problems, their troubles were multiplied because they were confronted from the beginning with the ticklish difficulty of understanding and expressing their faith in ever new and ever changing cultural settings.

The word *culture* here does not refer primarily to "high culture"—ballet and caviar and the opera, for example—but is used as anthropologists do to mean the whole way of life of a people. It includes their values, moral codes, religion, institutions, and their way of looking at themselves and at the universe. Every culture possesses all of these aspects, but they take different forms. For example, every culture has some way of teaching its young, but though in one culture a parent may teach a child a trade, in another, colleges and universities provide the necessary training. All cultures will have some kind of government and some form of civil marriage, but these take differing forms from culture to culture.

All the pieces of a given culture fit together in a consistent whole, a pattern. Because of this, all of a given culture's practices and beliefs make sense within that culture. The practices and beliefs fit together, though they may seem foolish or even harmful when viewed by an outsider—someone from another culture. Taken to extremes, this insight has led to an uncompromising cultural relativism, which does not allow for any meaningful cross-cultural dialogue. But there is an important truth: Every one of us is in large part a product of our culture, which shapes each of us and shapes how we view the world. I am a twenty-first-century, white, middle-class United States citizen. I see things the way white, middle-class United States citizens see things. This includes how I understand my Christian faith. Through effort and compassion I can transcend this culture and to some extent understand a Pakistani or a Native American, but only in a limited way. I cannot get out of my own skin and crawl into theirs. In school we read Edward Everett Hale's story *The Man without a Country*. It is difficult even to imagine a man without a culture.

From the earliest days of the Church until today, this problem of Christ and faith in tension with, yet connected to, culture has posed a difficult problem for Christianity, which understands itself as a universal faith that transcends cultural differences and applies equally to all people groups. When a person from one culture proclaims the Christian faith to members of another culture, the words in which the faith is stated and even the worldview that forms its setting must be translated into new ways of thinking to be relevant or to make sense to the new audience. But in doing so, there is the ever-present danger that, stated in a new framework, the original meaning of the statements of faith may become warped or even lost altogether. In abandoning the previous culturally accepted and culturally specific way of stating the Christian faith, the very tenets of the faith may be hidden or discarded. In one sense, the baby may get thrown out with the bath water.

To make matters worse, individuals listening to the Gospel message may not realize that their unique cultural context is different from that of the speaker, which affects their understanding of the Gospel. We tend to take for granted that our own culture's ways of looking at things are *truths*, not just beliefs. The less we realize how these ideas are formed, the stronger their hold on us may become.

The problem of being faithful to the original message while being relevant is always with us. It has been an obvious problem for missionaries who sometimes without thinking identify the Gospel with Western civilization. Certainly this identification often has been too easily accepted. We also are confronted by the fact that our culture is changing before our eyes as nations and people groups face the opportunities and challenges of modern science and technology. The agonizing battle between so-called traditionalists and modernists in the Church today is evidence enough of this ongoing cultural shift. Witness the deeply divisive battles over issues such as gay rights, life issues, feminism, and, of course, the question of how we should relate to the prevalent scientific worldview of our day.

What is true for us today was also a monumental problem for the Church in New Testament times. The difficulties the Early Church faced as it arrived at the accepted basics of the faith were compounded by life in a uniquely multicultural world. The earliest Christians found themselves imbedded in three differing, but overlapping, cultures: Jewish, Roman, and Greek.

Judaism

First-century Judaism was the cradle of Christianity. Jesus Himself was a Jew, as were all His disciples. Christianity inherited from Judaism a fierce dedication to monotheism—the worship of one God, Yahweh, the Creator of heaven and earth. Coupled with this dedication to monotheism was a strong moral code that Jews were expected to follow. Christians also believed that though Jesus' death and resurrection freed them from the observance of the Law, the power of the Holy Spirit at work in their lives resulted in obedience to the Law. Both Jews and first-century Christians differed from the citizens of the Gentile world that surrounded them. In this pagan culture there were many gods, and those who followed these gods were seldom under any kind of moral obligation. Actually, the pagan gods were not known for their high moral standards. Neither, in some cases, were their followers (Acts 15:20).

Judaism supplied the Early Christian Church with sacred writings and a belief that in these Scriptures God's will and His dealings with humanity were revealed. At first, the Jewish Scriptures were the only generally recognized holy books that the followers of Jesus could refer to as authoritative. And refer to them they did! In fact, the Hebrew Scriptures became a Christian book. For many believers, the events and the words of the prophets recorded in the Old Testament (the Jewish Scriptures) referred to Jesus Himself. The sacrifices practiced by the Israelites of the Old Testament were types of Jesus' sacrifice on the cross. Jesus Himself was speaking in the Psalms. Mention of the city of Jerusalem was understood by the earliest Christians as a reference to the church or to heaven.

The Early Christian Church did have its own holy books, which were writings about Jesus and letters from Paul and other apostles. Throughout the first centuries of the Church, there was considerable controversy over which of these writings could be called Scripture, as we shall see. But once there was general agreement concerning which Christian writings were inspired by the Holy Spirit, these documents, too, bore the seal of God's own authority.

With some exceptions, Judaism was exclusionary. First-century Jews had learned from bitter experience that corruption could infect their society through association with other cultures, their gods, and their pagan practices. Jews attempted to keep contact with the Gentile world to a minimum. The earliest followers of Jesus shared this attitude. Initially, only Jews were to be Christians; Gentiles need not apply.

This wall of exclusion was cracked only gradually. There were Jews, especially those living outside Palestine, who had been influenced by Greek (Hellenistic) culture. Their inclusion in the Church broadened the membership beyond Palestinian Jews. However, though they were Hellenists, they were still Jews.

Peter was the first apostle to baptize a Gentile into the Christian faith that would live among the Aramaic and Greek Jewish Christians. Peter was roundly criticized for bringing Cornelius into the body of Christ, but he made his case before the other apostles and prevailed. The door was now open to Gentile Christians. Eventually, more Gentiles joined the Way (Acts 10–11).

At this point Paul reenters the picture as a crucial figure within the Early Christian Church. He was tailor-made to initiate the transition from Jewish to Gentile Christianity. Paul was both a Jew and a citizen of the Roman Empire, though he was influenced enough by Hellenism to write in Greek. Thus all the main cultural influences of the first century were united in his person. With his keen mind, inexhaustible energy, and thoroughgoing dedication to the Christian faith, Paul was an ideal missionary. He went from synagogue to synagogue, proclaiming the Gospel to his fellow Jews, as well as to the Gentiles. Some who heard Paul preach and teach were baptized into the Christian faith; others were deeply offended by his words.

The Book of Acts describes a crucial event in Paul's changeover from a Jewish to a Gentile missionary. Paul was in Antioch of Pisidia, and as was his custom, he spoke at the synagogue and proclaimed the faith. Some Gentiles converted, but a number of the Jews, Paul's own people, not only rejected his message but also contradicted and reviled him. Paul and Barnabas boldly exclaimed: "It was necessary that the word of God be spoken first to you. Since you thrust it aside and judge yourselves unworthy of eternal life, behold, we are turning to the Gentiles. For so the Lord has commanded us, saying, 'I have made you a light for the Gentiles, that you may bring salvation to the ends of the earth'" (Acts 13:46–47). With his considerable talent and dedication, Paul now turned his mission efforts toward the Gentiles and became known as the apostle sent to the Gentiles, even as his own testimony suggests (Galatians 1:16).

As the number of Gentile converts grew within the Christian Church, the issue of culture soon raised its head. For example, some asked whether a Gentile convert to Christianity also needed to be a Jew. If the answer was yes, did male converts need to be circumcised? Did converts need to observe the Jewish dietary laws and other ceremonial laws? For some first-century Christians, the answer to all these questions was self-evident: "Of course they do!" The God of the Jews is the Father of the Lord Jesus. God's Laws have not changed; He intends that they be kept.

Paul was of an entirely different mind concerning circumcision and dietary and ceremonial laws. He took his stand on the doctrine of grace. According to Paul, no law saves us. It is God's grace that reconciles us to Himself, and this is received by faith, not by any human activity or observance of the Law. If it is faith that saves, then a person is a Christian by that faith, not by keeping the Jewish law or any other cultural prescription. Paul proclaimed, "There is neither Jew nor Greek, there is neither slave nor free, there is neither male nor female, for you are all one in Christ Jesus" (Galatians 3:28). Paul's openness to taking God's salvation to all people groups was based firmly on his insistence that we are justified by grace through faith.

Here, too, as the Book of Acts tells us, there was resentment, just as there had been when Peter welcomed Cornelius. But in their presentations of the case before the assembled apostles, both Paul and Peter testified to the central theme of justification alone through faith in Christ and received the approval of James and the assembly, based squarely on the Scriptures (Acts 15). Christianity could now arise from its Jewish cradle and be a universal faith. Before long the Gentiles constituted the majority within the Christian community. This victory not only opened the door to a vast throng of peoples, it also raised the serious question of how this Gospel was to be presented to, and heard by, individuals in new cultural settings; those who had little or no knowledge or concern for such concepts as the Messiah; or those who had little or no understanding of the rich Jewish heritage out of which Christianity grew.

The Roman Empire

If Judaism was the religious setting for primitive Christianity, the Roman Empire supplied the wider political context. Rome had begun as one of the many city-states scattered around the Mediterranean world. Gradually, by conquest and treaty, it was able to control all of Italy and eventually the entire Mediterranean shoreline. The Romans called it *mare nostrum*, "our lake." When General Pompey captured the city of Jerusalem in 63 BC, the ring was almost complete, and Palestine was annexed to the sphere of Rome.

During its period of expansion, dangerous cracks began to appear in the Roman social and governmental structures in the late Republic. The old guard—the patrician aristocracy, which was represented by the senate—tried to preserve law and order, as well as their own privileged status. Meanwhile, the commoner often was driven into deeper and deeper poverty—even into slavery.

The result was predictable. A series of civil wars erupted, and one leader after another arose to seize power in the name of "the people." Julius Caesar was the last of that line. He took over Rome, had himself declared dictator, and intimidated the senate. Members of the senate assassinated him in 44 BC.

Following Caesar's death, two men fought for the position of ruler of Rome. One man was Octavian, the other Anthony. Octavian defeated Anthony and his consort Cleopatra of Egypt at the battle of Actium in 31 BC, thus adding Egypt to Roman rule. Octavian made himself emperor and took the title "Augustus." What was left of the Roman Republic was now dead; the Roman Empire, with an emperor, had begun.

Christianity and this empire began at about the same time. One may recall the following from the events of the birth of Jesus recorded in Luke's Gospel: "In those days a decree went out from Caesar Augustus that all the world should be registered " (Luke 2:1). But the relationship between the Roman world and the fledgling church would be a checkered one at best—at worst, it was a disaster.

The Romans felt they could take well-deserved pride in their mastery of the empire. They believed the various nations had come under their sway not only because of good fortune but also because as Romans they possessed certain virtues, such as courage, loyalty, and devotion to duty. The Romans ruled over a motley collection of tribes, languages, cultures, religions, and forms of government. They did it through Roman law, which applied not just to specific groups of people, but to everywhere Rome ruled. Of course, the laws were backed up by the muscle of the Roman legions. Through legal and military means, the Romans brought peace and order—the *Pax Romana*—to many regions that previously had been beset by chaos and war.

By and large, the Romans ruled their vast multicultural empire with a laudable spirit of toleration. If you paid your taxes and avoided any hint of rebellion against the emperor, you were allowed to keep your beliefs and practices. The Romans were proud of their religious toleration; they not only allowed various peoples to keep their native gods and goddesses, but these also might be added to the Roman pantheon or amalgamated with existing Roman gods. Religious pluralism and toleration were in full bloom.

This practice of religious toleration makes it difficult to understand why Christians were singled out for persecution. Although there was no consistent pattern of persecution everywhere and at all times in the Roman Empire, occasionally an emperor would decree a universal persecution throughout the empire. Most of the harassment of Christians occurred sporadically in a particular province and for a specific length of time. But Christians never felt safe for long. Their churches could be destroyed, their Bibles confiscated, and they could be enslaved, imprisoned, or, as we know from history, thrown to the lions.

A whole host of false charges were leveled against the followers of Christ as justification for persecution: They ate body and blood, so they were cannibals. They held part of their worship services in secret, so they must be guilty of some sort of gross immorality. They refused to participate in public ceremonies honoring the gods who protected the Roman Empire, so they were atheists. Perhaps the most damning accusation against the early Christians was that they were traitors—a disloyal lot who likely were plotting the overthrow the Roman government. After all, these Christians had gotten off to a bad start. Their leader, Jesus, had been condemned to death by a Roman governor, perhaps as a Jewish revolutionary because He claimed to be the "King of the Jews." Romans did not like to think that their governors made mistakes in dealing with the provincials. On top of belief in Jesus, the Christians absented themselves from participation in civil ceremonies and adamantly refused to perform sacrifices to the quasi-divine spirit or "genius" that was supposed to guide the Roman emperor and, with him, the Empire. This is a clear example of

Christians refusing to make peace with the surrounding culture as they attempted to obey God rather than man.

Although the Romans were tolerant of various religions, they were suspicious of new religions that could be a mask for crime and insurrection within a particular territory. Therefore, if the Christians wanted to be accepted, they had to claim some kind of antiquity. They could do this only by proclaiming that they were a continuation of Judaism, the "true" Israel. Unfortunately, this did not work either. It only made matters worse because the Jews themselves were in rebellion against Rome during the first decades after Jesus' death, resurrection, and ascension. Finally, the Jews were suppressed by military might in AD 70 and AD 135. Christianity's distaste for recognizing its Jewish roots at this time marks an important step in the separation of the Christians from the Jews.

During the second century, a group of Christian writers arose that was collectively known as the Apologists. (An "apology" is not a statement of contrition or repentance; it is a statement or defense of a position.) This group attempted to answer the charges that had been made against the believers in Jesus. The Apologists proclaimed that Christians were not subversive because they were taught to respect authority. They were not immoral because they, more than others, knew that the eye of God was upon them. Concerning the pantheon of Roman gods, the Apologists admitted themselves and their fellow Christians to be atheists, but not atheists in relation to the one God, who is the true God. The writings of the Apologists usually were addressed to a specific Roman emperor or to other influential Romans. The documents did little good with respect to their accusers and probably were not even read by those to whom they were sent. Accusations and persecutions continued.

Hellenism

As it expanded, Rome conquered Greece, but to a great extent, the Roman mind was conquered by Greek thought. The Greeks thought of their conquerors as little more than barbarians, and the Romans had to admit that they were faced with a culture that was intellectually superior to theirs.

The Greeks (Hellenes) had every reason to take pride in their history and culture (and they still do). From ancient Greece we have the literary classics of the ancient world, including Homer and his epics, as well as playwrights like Aeschylus, Sophocles, Euripides, and Aristophanes. We receive from the Greeks the first two important historians, Herodotus and Thucydides. Perhaps the greatest Greek claim to fame is the legacy of philosophical thinkers such as Thales (the "father of philosophy") and the great philosophers of Athens: Socrates, Plato, and Aristotle, who are still studied as giants in the realm of human culture and thought. Hundreds of years before Roman legions marched into Greece, Greek culture had spread throughout the eastern Mediterranean world—into Persia, Palestine, Egypt, and even to the borders of India through the military efforts of Alexander the Great.

Alexander, called the Great, was the son of Philip II, the king of Macedon (or Macedonia). Alexander had been tutored by the great Aristotle, with one result being that he quickly fell in love with all things Greek. He and his father conquered Greece, and when Philip was assassinated, Alexander became king at age 20. Now in power, he set his mind to defeat the Persians, who were the ancient enemies of the Greeks. Although drastically outnumbered and fighting in enemy territory, Alexander defeated Darius and the Persian Empire in a series of brilliant battles that have placed him deservedly among the great generals of history. Alexander went on to add many other lands of the area from modern Turkey and Egypt to the borders of India, the area we now call the Middle East, to his trophy case. All this he accomplished in little more than a decade. Alexander died in Babylon in 323 BC at age 33.

Alexander not only conquered a huge empire, but he also was a true cultural imperialist and insisted on sharing his beloved Greek culture with the peoples under his rule. As he traveled he founded a number of cities that would become centers from which the Hellenistic culture would radiate. Appropriately enough, these cities were named "Alexandria." One of them, in Egypt, eventually would rival and even outdo Athens in the realm of intellectual prowess and respect.

After Alexander's death, his empire was divided among his generals and became what has been called the Hellenistic Empires. The generals continued Alexander's program of sharing, and sometimes enforcing, Greek culture upon captive nations. Their efforts were to a great extent successful. Greek thought, gods, architecture, games, and other aspects of Greek culture mixed with indigenous customs. The resulting amalgam is called "Hellenism," that is, "Greekism."

Hellenistic thought made its impact everywhere, especially among the educated. Greek became the *lingua franca* or common tongue of the Mediterranean world and beyond. Probably the closest thing in the modern era would be the impact of American culture upon much of the world. Chinese children learn English. Students in Moscow wear Dallas Cowboy's T-shirts. Kentucky Fried Chicken and McDonald's outlets can be found almost everywhere. Some wholeheartedly embrace this American culture; others resist it. Regardless of opinion, it cannot be avoided. In the ancient world, as now, the superimposition of one culture upon another tends to be disruptive. When, based in the Middle East, the Hellenistic king Antiochus IV tried to enforce his culture by outlawing Jewish practices and mandating pagan ones, the Jews began a wholesale rebellion. For about a century, this small but courageous people resisted the powerful Hellenistic kingdom during a period some historians call the War of the Maccabees. During these years, the Jews sometimes kept the Greeks at bay; sometimes they even drove them from Palestine. Ultimately, the

Romans ended the whole affair when Pompey and his legions marched into Jerusalem in 63 BC.

Despite their best efforts, the Jews could not completely resist the allure and power of the influential Greek culture. This was particularly true of those Jews who lived outside Palestine—and there were a great number of them. The Jews in Alexandria, Egypt, for example, had forgotten their Hebrew language to such an extent that they petitioned the rabbis in Jerusalem to prepare for them a Greek version of the Scriptures (what is now the Old Testament). This would become known as the Septuagint. Even the Jews in Jerusalem could not entirely buck the trend, and Hellenistic influences were found there as well.

One of the striking features of the Hellenism of this time was the continuation of the great Greek tradition of philosophy. New "schools" of philosophy, or ways of thinking, grew up throughout the Roman Empire. These schools had considerable influence on the thinking of the educated class. They represented the best "science" of the day, and the Christian community would have to deal with them as well. This was true not only because believers in Christ wanted their message to be relevant to hearers who adhered to a particular school of thought but also because these new believers themselves were influenced in their thought patterns by these schools. We will discuss some of these schools of philosophy later, though here we will take a brief look at one of them—Stoicism.

The philosophical school known as Stoicism was one of the most influential in the ancient world. Cicero, the great Roman statesman and author, and the Roman emperor Marcus Aurelius were both Stoics. Although there were nuances and variations of belief within Stoicism, its main tenets are clear enough: The universe is the supreme being or "god," what we today call pantheism. Stoics did not believe that god made the universe; rather, they held that god *is* the universe. The physical world is god's body; the beautiful order of the world reveals god's mind. The Stoics named this mind *logos*, Greek for "word." Just as our words are physical vibrations in the air that also express our inner thoughts, so the *logos*, which reveals the inner rationality of the Stoic's "god."

According to the Stoics, god is rational, but so are human beings. Thus we humans have something of the *logos* in us that enables us to see the order of nature. There are a number of important corollaries to this: First, because we all have something of god in us, we are all children of the same god and brothers and sisters of one another. Second, because we all share the same basic reason, and law is the social expression of reason, we can all be governed by the same laws, a helpful thought for those trying to govern a vast multicultural empire. Another corollary, and an important one for the Stoics, is that we can be at peace among the evils of the world by using our reason to understand the forces of nature. Thus we can see that evils are only part of a greater good. Thus Stoics were well-known for their tranquility in the face of adversity.

Could Christians possibly make common cause with this school of philosophy? Clearly there are some attractive elements in it. In fact, the path had already been cleared for just such an attempt at melding Christianity and Stoicism by Philo, a Hellenistic Jew. He attempted to identify the Word of God in Scripture—which had already taken on an identity of its own in some Jewish circles—with the *logos* of the Stoics.

We now turn back to the Christian Apologists and their attempts to relate their faith to the best in their culture. Justin Martyr, arguably the most important Apologist, attempted to relate to his hearers by beginning where they were. When addressing a Jew, he emphasized that Jesus had fulfilled Jewish prophecy. But when addressing the educated and sophisticated Hellenists, Justin related his faith to the *logos*, the seed of reason in people that finds its perfection and complete unity in Christ, as he did in Chapters 8 and 10 of his *Second Apology*.[2] Although Justin previously had found Stoicism lacking, its concepts had become so entrenched in the philosophical landscape that the concept of *logos* was hard to avoid and also lent itself to his apology. We may recall that the Gospel of John had already insisted that "in the beginning was the Word [*Logos* in the original Greek] . . . and the Word [again, *Logos*] was made flesh" (John 1:1, 14).

Justin proclaimed that Jesus was in fact the Word made flesh. He said that because we as humans are rational, we all have some share in this *Logos*, some more than others. Socrates, for example, had more than the usual share. But it was the Word in its fullness—the Word as *its very self*—who dwelt in Jesus Christ and only in Him. According to Justin, great thinkers throughout history had sought this truth but had failed to attain it. Yet their searching entitled the great and sincere ones, like Socrates, to be called Christians before Christ.

In his attempt to come to terms with his culture, Justin had opened a pathway for Christian thinkers to come. From now on, many of them would equate the Son with the Word and with all that might be implied in that identification. Some, like Tertullian in the third century, would reject such a dalliance with pagan philosophy. He would set up the comparison between the Christian, properly a citizen of Jerusalem, and the citizens of the world: Rome, Athens, and the like. So, what has Athens to do with Jerusalem? Tertullian's implied answer was: Nothing at all. That approach appears repeatedly in a number of his works, including the *Apology*, *The Chaplet*, *A Treatise on the Soul* and *The Five Books Against Marcion.*[3]

Of one thing we may be sure: Justin's attempt to convince the Roman authorities did not succeed. This great Apologist's title was "Martyr" because he was put to death for his faith.

The Gnostic and Marcionite Controversies: Irenaeus

N ot much is known about the details of Irenaeus's life. He was a Greek-speaking bishop of Lyons, located in southern France, who lived during the second century AD. Evidently, Irenaeus was born in the Middle East. According to Irenaeus's writings, it was important to him that he had known Polycarp personally. Polycarp was a second-century bishop and martyr (d. about AD 155) who had known the apostle John. Irenaeus was elevated to the Episcopal chair at Lyons upon the death of the previous bishop of that area, who himself had been martyred. The manner and year of Irenaeus's own death are unknown, though it was probably around the year AD 200 that he also died as a martyr.

It is generally agreed that Irenaeus was the most important Christian thinker of the Early Christian Church as it existed in the second century, which was the century immediately following the ministry and lives of the apostles and the writing of the documents now known collectively as the New Testament. Irenaeus was the first to attempt a comprehensive, integrated presentation of the Christian faith. Together with the fact that he stands so close to New Testament figures, this attempt gives added weight to his thoughts. His influence on the Eastern Orthodox Church has been immense. Western thinkers, particularly in the modern age, have given Irenaeus little attention, and when they have, they often have been highly critical.

The most important source of Irenaeus's thoughts on the Christian faith can be found in his massive work usually referred to as *Against Heresies*, for which the full title is *The Detection and Overthrow of the Pretended but False Gnosis* (knowledge). It is unfortunate that this work, originally written in Greek, exists only in a Latin translation. Only limited sections of the Greek have been preserved. A much shorter work, the *Demonstration of Apostolic Preaching*, exists only in a rather tortured literal Armenian translation of the Greek original. In these writings, Irenaeus dedicated himself to opposing what he believed were threats to the central teachings of the Christian faith: the doctrines of Marcion and the Gnostics. Irenaeus countered these teachings by using the Scriptures—which by his time were much like the Bible most of us use today—and by promoting the worship and faith traditions handed down from the apostles, an apostolic succession to which he considered himself an heir.

Gnosticism

One question that can be asked by sincere people, and indeed often is asked, is whether God, the all-powerful and perfect God, can be the creator of this flawed and problematic universe? Or is this world the work of some lower, inferior being—Plato called this lower being the *demiurge*—which infused the world with ignorance and even malice? Can the Creator who placed us in this world ever be the Savior who delivers us from the human predicament, namely, sin and death? Such questions have been asked throughout history, and the answer often has been a resounding no.

Such was the reaction of those groups and individuals who have been labeled as Gnostics. For them it was inconceivable that the all-powerful, omniscient God could place us in this fix. Instead, the demiurge put us in this world with its mixture of matter and spirit. The God who is above all could never do such a thing; He is pure spirit. Gnostics also believed that humanity's true kinship is with God Himself, thus our true home is in the heavenly places. Some divine being higher than the world-creator must come to save us by his grace and reveal to us our true nature and the means of ascending back to that spiritual home. For many Gnostics, this savior could not be a flesh-and-blood human being or he also would be encumbered by and tainted with created matter. He could not have the same digestive system as we do, for example, nor could he truly have been born or suffered or died. In some other form Jesus only appeared to live, suffer, and die. This particular tenet of Gnosticism is called docetism (from *doceo*, "to appear").

Gnosticism was a potent force in the late first century and throughout the second century. Already we see that 2 Thessalonians 2:3f., 1 John 2:22, 2 John 7 and some related texts in Revelation suggest some kind of Gnostic encroachment on the Christian Church. But it is difficult to pin down exactly what Gnosticism entails because the philosophy was diverse and came from rather obscure origins. Its overlapping and ambiguous teachings made it especially difficult to identify core or common beliefs among the various Gnostic groups. Irenaeus said that he could better argue with the Gnostics if only they could agree with one another. He also said their differing schools seemed to grow up like mushrooms. One only has to read through the hundreds of pages of Irenaeus's descriptions of the differing complex cosmologies of the Gnostics to agree with him.

For centuries the greatest source of information about the Gnostics have been the writings of Irenaeus, as well as those of Tertullian and Hippolytus, two other "anti-Gnostic fathers." In the

1940s, however, an ancient library was uncovered at Nag Hammadi in upper Egypt that provided scholars with a treasure trove of new materials about such splinter groups within the Early Christian Church. Unfortunately, this archaeological discovery has also compounded the confusion about which groups can be called Gnostic and to which variety of Gnosticism they should be assigned, if indeed there is any commonality at all. Thus it is dangerous to make sweeping generalizations about the Gnostics; indeed, Irenaeus is careful to treat adherents of Gnosticism separately. Yet there are certain points on which all Gnostics, or at least a great number of them, did agree. Several scholars have attempted summaries of Gnostic views, for example:

- Gnostics "were concerned with the salvation of the inner, spiritual man . . . chained to the body. By *gnosis* [knowledge], which is brought to men from above for his salvation, he can be freed."[1]

- Gnostics "all united in assuming that, so far as religion was concerned, the material was the antithesis to the spiritual. Material existence was, if not the active enemy of spiritual living, at least inert, unprofitable, and a hampering burden."[2]

- Gnosticism, "viewed as a chapter in the history of Christian doctrine . . . may be defined as a system which taught the cosmic redemption of the spirit through knowledge."[3]

Michael Allen Williams has gone so far as to suggest that we drop the category "Gnostic" altogether and replace it with "biblical demiurgy," which captures the ideas of those who considered themselves Christian but believed the world to have been created by the demiurge.[4] Before such a decision can be made, much more research needs to be done.[5] If we think present-day Christianity is confusing with all its denominations, sects, and variants, we might take some small comfort when we look at the chaos in the Early Church.

Despite an overwhelming variety of teachings, there were some common themes among the Gnostics, at least as Irenaeus saw them. And Irenaeus found these common beliefs to be intolerable. First, the Gnostics were dedicated seekers after salvation. They believed that knowledge (*gnosis* in the Greek) is the way to salvation. Knowledge cannot only clarify the nature of the problem, but it is also the way to overcome the problem. It reveals to human beings a true self-understanding, as well as an understanding of the way home—the way to reunion with the true God, who is above all. The Savior, the Christ, is the one who gives us this knowledge.

Good enough! But as we have already noted, this salvation takes place in the context of a worldview in which God cannot be the creator and in which Christ cannot be fully human. He received nothing material, for the material is incapable of being saved. For some, the human Jesus was crucified, but not Christ, or Sophia (Wisdom).[6]

Further, the insistence of the Gnostics on the complete separation of God and the world led them to proclaim—or invent, as Irenaeus saw it—a vast host of intermediate heavenly creatures that stood between God and this evil world. These beings were placed in an elaborate scheme in which emanations, the spiritual unions or copulations of "eons" and their respective deficiencies in this somewhat androgynous and incestuous genealogy were arrayed downward, in step after step, from God to the lowest spiritual being, the demiurge, who, as we have seen, created this world. This let the "true God," as they believed it, "off the hook" as far as creation is concerned. Irenaeus describes the system of Valentinus, one of the most important or at least one of the best-known Gnostics, as propounded by Ptolemaeus, a follower of Valentinus. Although not all the Gnostics subscribed to this exact description, Robert Grant's example can be considered fairly typical:

> The one pre-existent Aeon, Pre-Beginning or Forefather or Depth, emitted a Beginning of all into his companion

Thought/Grace/Silence, who then bore Mind/Only-Begotten/Father/Beginning. Truth was emitted with him to compose the first tetrad: Depth, Silence, Mind, Truth. A series of emissions then began when Only-Begotten produced Logos and Life and they Produced Man and Church, making up the Ogdoad, and then ten more. Man and Church emitted another twelve, the last of which was Sophia. These thirty aeons made up the Pleroma.

Sophia "leaped forth" from her place with her consort Willed and experienced passion in her desire to comprehend the incomprehensible Father. She would have been dissolved had not Limit stopped her and made her return to herself, at the same time crucifying her Desire. When Sophia was restored to the Pleroma, Only-Begotten emitted another pair, Christ and the Holy Spirit, to teach how the Father is incomprehensible and what the nature of spiritual "rest" is.

Sophia's desire, also known as Achamoth, was lost below, but Christ extended himself to her through the Cross and gave her shape as she suffered many emotions (1.4.2). Christ then returned to the Pleroma but sent the Paraclete, the Savior, to her. The Savior enabled her to shape three kinds of entities: material (from her passion), psychic (from her conversion), and spiritual (from her essential nature).[7]

It should be noted that all of what has just been described is nonhistorical. It exists in the heavenly places, the *pleroma*, the fullness or perfection. The world as we experience it has not yet been created. Although the terms are those usually used for events and persons in our history—Christ, church, etc.—for the Gnostics these entities were timeless realities, of which earthly persons and events are only types or shadows. But Grant continues:

> Out of the psychic nature she fashioned the Demiurge,
> who preserved the image of Only-Begotten and was the
> maker of all psychic and material beings. He shaped
> seven heavens, which are angels, and dwells above them.
> He ignorantly thought he made them, but Achamoth
> projected them first.[8]

For readers who make their way through this rather thick mythological soup, at least one thing should be clear: The Gnostic cosmology was constructed to separate the ultimate God from this universe and to absolve him from any blame in making it. The present world, made by the demiurge, is the result of a number of falls or deficiencies.

It is interesting to notice that at the same time the Gnostics are removing God from all contact with the physical world, they are simultaneously dissolving the divine/human distinction by making us the result of a series of emanations from God. Our soul, and even more our spirit, belongs in the divine realm with God. Our spiritual natures are, in some sense, divine. In fact, being related to the highest divinity stands at the core of much of Gnostic thinking about salvation. For many Gnostics, the creation of humans left some of us with no more than a physical nature. These folks probably can never achieve salvation. Others have not only a physical but also a spiritual nature, thus they can rise above the merely carnal. Still others, the true Gnostics, are blessed with a spark of that highest God within them, thus they can be saved simply by using the right techniques to realize their true selves and rise to their proper home. Often there was a kind of conversion experience proclaimed in Gnosticism, though it typically was a realization of what was already true—humanity's divine nature—rather than any real change in the person or healing of a deep-seated spiritual illness.

Furthermore, Irenaeus saw that this view cuts Christianity off from history and keeps it in the eternal realms. According to Irenaeus, the Gnostics claim that the maker and creator of the world—the demiurge—has always been known to us, but the true God, who is definitely different from the demiurge, remained unknown until revealed to us by the savior. The creator is not the savior; the savior is not the creator.

The ethics of the Gnostics tended to flow from their theology. Asceticism was their usual practice. Adherents were discouraged from eating meat. Marriage was not encouraged either because the begetting of children would condemn more souls to imprisonment in bodies. A few Gnostics evidently took an entirely different tack. To show their contempt for the body, they felt free to use it in all ways imaginable. But this was probably a small sect within the larger movement. However, sweeping generalizations should be avoided because most Gnostics were not entirely consistent. Both extremes tended to live what could only be termed normal lives.

Although some Gnostic views may appear bizarre, encrusted as they were with elaborate cosmic myths, they had great power in the ancient world: The religion of the Gnostics proclaimed the salvation of the inner person. Likewise it allowed the believer to consider historical matters unimportant for salvation. This teaching has some attractiveness even today—simply witness everything from contemporary "spiritual" religion to the work of Rudolph Bultmann and others in "demythologizing" that, with other efforts, attempts to separate the Jesus of history from the Christ of faith.

The Gnostics clearly believed in God's grace, but they held to it in such a way that it denied both the goodness of creation and the historicity of the incarnation. For Irenaeus, this was intolerable. It cut the heart out of the historic Christian faith.

Marcion

Another movement that Irenaeus saw as a threat to the Early Church was that of Marcion and his followers.[9] Although he started from different concerns and premises than the Gnostics,

Marcion's results were similar to theirs in important respects. Marcion was a dedicated follower of the teachings of the apostle Paul, especially in the matter of justification by faith and freedom from the Law. His problem was that he could not reconcile the God of the Old Testament with that of the God of the New Testament. To Marcion it seemed impossible to believe that the one who placed us in this painful world and the one who rescues us from it can be the same. Nor can the one who adds to our burdens by giving us the Law be the same one who frees us from the power of the Law. Marcion concluded that there are two gods: the higher God, the merciful Father of our Lord Jesus Christ, whom he calls "the Loving Stranger"; and the lower, creator god, who at best is just, but not good, and at worst is evil. So Marcion, like the Gnostics, denied that the true God is the Creator and also refused to believe that the Christ really came in the flesh. A church council eventually condemned Marcion and his followers in AD 144.[10]

Irenaeus the Gnostic

When Irenaeus took up his pen to counter the Gnostic view of reality and of the Christian faith, he was well aware that he would have to submit his own *gnosis*. Recall that the full title of what we call *Against Heresies* is *The Detection and Overthrow of the Pretended False Gnosis*. Irenaeus would have to show that his own understanding of God and the human race was itself rational, not false, that it made sense, as well as being in the true succession of the teaching of the apostles. The point has often been missed of just how close Irenaeus is to the Gnostics in this regard. In contesting with them, he declares: "True knowledge is [that which consists in] the teaching of the Apostles."[11] Time after time, and in one context after another, Irenaeus stresses how knowledge is key to salvation. It is crucial for him to show that the true Father, whom the Gnostics claim to be unknown, has been revealed through nature and through Scripture so we may know Him.

Of course, the main point behind this approach is that what is known, what is revealed, is far different from what the Gnostics teach. Irenaeus's resulting proclamation of the faith, in both its form and its content, ended up being almost totally opposite from that of his opponents. On almost every point, Irenaeus asserted beliefs that were 180 degrees distant from those of the Gnostics, as we shall see. But this does not mean that he composed his views merely as a foil to Gnosticism. Instead, he had his own standpoint, his own set of beliefs already worked out, and from this perspective Irenaeus took his stand against the Gnostics. He well may have sharpened his ideas and elaborated them as a result of these controversies, but his whole system of thought is so rich, so complex, yet circling around so few major ideas, that it cannot be only a response to others.

There are two foci around which Irenaeus's entire thought orbits, and they must both be kept in mind if we want to grasp the richness of his theology. The first of these is his concept of the *oikoumene* or "arrangement," or as it is usually translated, the dispensation. This same word refers to how persons arrange their household finances. For Irenaeus it is the whole way in which God arranges His universe and all that is in it, from creation to the consummation on the Last Day and everything in between. God's goodness, love, and grace are displayed in this dispensation. Even the disruption caused by human sin is accounted for because, according to Irenaeus, God in His foreknowledge saw that this would occur and made accommodation for it. The second focus is the recapitulation, in which, as the central act of the dispensation, Jesus Christ unites with His creation as a real human being. Taking his cue from Paul, Irenaeus sees Christ as the Second Adam, who experiences all that the first Adam did but this time does it right, giving humanity a new head, a restored image and likeness, and a new start.[12]

As we have said, Irenaeus proclaimed his own *gnosis* in contrast to that of the Gnostics. Two things should be noted concerning this *gnosis*. First, it was necessary for Irenaeus to establish that his views had just as much authority—and more—than those of his opponents. The Gnostics justified their system of thought by insisting their message had been passed to them by means of secret communications from the earliest apostles. Irenaeus countered them with a constant reference to Scripture and by his well-known reference to apostolic succession. His citations of the Old Testament, particularly in *The Demonstration*, were constant, and Irenaeus also quoted Paul and John frequently, as well as the Synoptic Gospels. In opposing the fanciful Gnostic interpretation of Scripture, Irenaeus insists that it can be understood only out of itself. It is the Gnostics who try to explain Scripture from outside itself.

It was also of the highest importance to Irenaeus that his message and his authority had been handed down to him through an open—not secret—succession of teachings from the apostles themselves all the way to the catholic bishops of his time, including himself. "We are in a position to reckon up those who were by the apostles instituted bishops in the Churches, and [to demonstrate] the succession of these men to our own times . . . also [by pointing out] the faith preached to men, which comes down to our time by means of the successions of the bishops."[13] This tradition is the bearer of true knowledge and has continued unaltered. The Gnostics cannot claim this firmly rooted message. "[N]either the prophets, nor the apostles, nor the Lord Christ in His own person, did acknowledge any other Lord or God, but the God and Lord supreme: the prophets and the apostles confessing the Father and the Son; but naming no other as God, and confessing no other as Lord: and the Lord Himself handing down to His disciples, that He, the Father, is the only God and Lord, who alone is God and ruler of all."[14]

Irenaeus approached matters of faith from an entirely different perspective than the Gnostics. In keeping with much of the "science" of their day, the Gnostics resorted to elaborate cosmological speculations to explain their position, as we have already seen. Irenaeus, on the other hand, had little or nothing to do with such philosophical musings. According to Irenaeus, Scripture does not teach us everything, and it is the height of arrogance to try to understand what God does tell us. Such speculation only distracts us from faith and love. These matters should be left to God.[15]

But more important than his rejection of this arrogance is Irenaeus's firm conviction that humans are historical beings. Our identity and our relationship to God simply cannot be grasped through contemplating events in a timeless *pleroma*. We live in time and grow in it. The human drama is played out entirely on a temporal and spatial plane. In other words, Irenaeus wants to bring the whole divine-human drama down to earth. Furthermore, God Himself has organized His dealings with man in terms of this historical drama. To reduce it to truths grounded on the speculative contemplation of a reality outside of time and space as we know it is to ignore the conflict in which we are embroiled and to evacuate the historical occurrence of Jesus Christ, the center of our faith.[16]

Irenaeus's insistence on grounding the divine-human relationship in history allowed him—even demanded of him—that he express his own *gnosis* in different terms than that of his opponents. In keeping with this, the method or principles guiding the structure of his arguments was almost always literary, particularly drawing on the skills of writers noted for their prowess in rhetoric and the effective structure of arguments. Such methods did not depend on certain assertions made by any particular school of thought within the philosophical systems of his day. He was quite impatient with cosmological speculations; instead, Irenaeus constantly resorted to an understanding of things based upon a narrative that shows progress in time and that has its own inner logic—a beginning, middle, and end. Thus he was equally concerned to place his drama within the flesh-and-blood history of this real world, rather than in the mythological goings-on of the supposed upper realms. The entire human drama of creation, fall, and redemption is played out on an historical, not a cosmic, screen. It is interesting to note that most of the Early Church fathers who followed in Irenaeus's path also made important use of rhetorical methodologies, despite the fact that many also were given to occasional flights of philosophical speculation.

This approach of Irenaeus enabled him to focus less on an analysis of the causes of evil and to concentrate more on its cure. In treating the matter in this way, he sets the stage for the great majority of Christian thinkers through the ages.

The Drama of Salvation

A short summary of the drama of salvation as seen by Irenaeus can be expressed as follows: God created human beings for happiness, that is, for life and for immortality or union with Himself (which is the same thing as life). But being deceived by the serpent (whom Irenaeus equates with Satan), human beings disobeyed God. When they fell away from communion with God, they lost their chance to progress toward this union. They simultaneously fell into sin, decay, and death. Having obeyed Satan, human beings become his captives and cannot escape from slavery to Satan and to all of the evils that accompany this captivity.

Yet God is merciful. He initiates human salvation through the incarnation of His Word, Jesus Christ. By human obedience and divine power, Jesus Christ is able to defeat the captor (Satan) and free the captives. Jesus does this by "recapitulating" the human experience. He is the Second Adam who successfully endures every stage of our existence, thus undoing and canceling the disobedience of the first Adam. Having had the true God and the possibilities of human communion with God revealed to us, the human family is now free to dominate evil rather than be dominated by it, to live righteously, and to progress toward immortality and incorruptibility.

God

Both Irenaeus and the Gnostics insist that the highest God is beyond all human language and understanding. But in Irenaeus's mind, it is not he but the Gnostics who rob God of His true exaltedness by teaching that He emanates downward—one might even say "trickles downward"—through a series of stages or deficiencies into that world from which they try to keep Him separated. Irenaeus will have none of this. For him there is what we would today call an "infinite qualitative distinction" between God and all creation, including humans. God is the Creator; man is created. God is perfect in every respect; we are infinitely inferior to Him. To speak of any deficiencies in God is utter blasphemy.[17]

It is worthwhile to note that though Irenaeus places salvation in an ever-closer relationship between God and the human person, he never blurs the divine-human distinction. We are part of creation—perhaps the most important part—but creatures through and through. We must never forget it.

According to Irenaeus, emanations from God are unthinkable because God is an absolute unity. In reaction to the belief that *Zoe*, or life, is the sixth stage of descent, Irenaeus insists that these attributes are not part of some scale of descent but are only names of perfections that always exist in God. Separating such things as the Word from the being of God only shows that the Gnostics are trying to apply human categories to God, an act that remains impossible for Irenaeus.[18]

According to Irenaeus, any attempt to separate God from His thought and Word and life and Christ comes from the grossly mistaken attempt to understand Him in terms taken from human psychology. Irenaeus's insistence on the unity of God is extremely strong. The Word is the Creator, one of God's hands. Irenaeus's untiring emphasis on the unity of God accentuates his conviction that it is God who both created and redeemed the world, neither an emanation nor an angel nor a defect. He is willing to call God the demiurge but insists that this demiurge is the highest God and no other.[19] That all things were made through the Word and that the Word is absolutely God shows that God is directly involved in His world. Against Marcion, who divides the just god from the good god, Irenaeus is able to affirm that they are the same God. The Savior is the Creator; the Creator is the Savior. He is merciful, just, and patient.[20]

Two important truths result from this insistence that the good God created this world that the Gnostics and Marcionites condemn as evil. First, creation is not an evil prison for the soul. Rather, it is a gift. We see that it is grace in the sense that it is given freely, without condition, though it is not "grace" in the specific sense of salvation in Christ. God, who needed nothing, created Adam to have someone to whom to give His benefits. This cannot be separated from the second point: that God is revealed in nature and in His actions with the children of Israel. The Old Testament patriarchs and prophets knew God. Although they could not fathom Him in His greatness, they did know Him in His love. Man needs communion with God, and quoting the Gospel of John, Irenaeus says, "You did not choose me but I chose you."[21]

The Human Family

Humans, of course, are part of God's creation. In fact, we are its apex. We are to be the rulers of the earth. Even the angels were to be our servants. Everything was created for our benefit. Creation is made for humans, not humans for creation.[22]

But as great as we are, we cannot be compared to God.

> And in this respect God differs from man, that God indeed makes, but man is made; and truly, He who makes is always the same; but that which is made must receive both beginning, and middle, and addition, and increase. And God does indeed create after a skilful manner, while, [as regards] man, he *is* created skilfully. God also is truly perfect in all things, Himself equal and sim-

ilar to Himself, as He is all light, and all mind, and all substance, and the fount of all good; but man receives advancement and increase towards God.

If, however, any one say, "What then? Could not God have exhibited man as perfect from beginning?" let him know that, inasmuch as God is indeed always the same and unbegotten as respects Himself, all things are possible to Him. But created things must be inferior to Him who created them, from the very fact of their later origin; for it was not possible for things recently created to have been uncreated. But inasmuch as they are not uncreated, for this very reason do they come short of the perfect. Because, as these things are of later date, so are they infantile; so are they unaccustomed to, and unexercised in, perfect discipline.

. . . God had power at the beginning to grant perfection to man; but as the latter was only recently created, he could not possibly have received it, or even if he had received it, could he have contained it, or containing it, could he have retained it. It was for this reason that the Son of God, although He was perfect, passed through the state of infancy in common with the rest of mankind, partaking of it thus not for His own benefit, but for that of the infantile stage of man's existence, in order that man might be able to receive Him.

. . . For from the very fact of these things having been created, [it follows] that they are not uncreated; but by their continuing in being throughout a long course of ages, they shall receive a faculty of the Uncreated, through the gratuitous bestowal of eternal existence upon them by God. And thus in all things God has the pre-eminence, who alone is uncreated, the first of all things, and the primary cause of the existence of all, while all other things remain under God's subjection.

> But being in subjection to God is continuance in immortality, and immortality is the glory of the uncreated One.

> But since created things are various and numerous, they are indeed well fitted and adapted to the whole creation; yet, when viewed individually, are mutually opposite and inharmonious, just as the sound of the lyre, which consists of many and opposite notes, gives rise to one unbroken melody, through means of the interval which separates each one from the others. The lover of truth therefore ought not to be deceived by the interval between each note, nor should he imagine that one was due to one artist and author, and another to another, nor that one person fitted the treble, another the bass, and yet another the tenor strings; but he should hold that one and the same person [formed the whole], so as to prove the judgment, goodness, and skill exhibited in the whole work and [specimen of] wisdom.[23]

In other words, we are incurably historical beings. By God's grace, we will grow into greater and greater fellowship with God, but the distinction between Creator and creature will never be overcome. Irenaeus never tires of emphasizing the childlikeness of humanity—the smallness of man in his created state and his need for growth.[24]

Essential to our created nature is our *physical* nature. As opposed to the Gnostics, who want to separate humans into parts, Irenaeus stressed humans as whole beings—totalities, including bodies. It is not that the bodies are evil or that the soul ever exists separated from the body. Rather, Irenaeus insists that soul and body are righteous or sin together, will be rewarded or punished together, and will rise together. He continues by reasoning that, when Paul tells us that flesh and blood cannot inherit the kingdom, he cannot mean that the physical body will not inherit it.[25] He refers, instead, to the carnal actions that turn man toward sin and deprive him of life. Indeed, if the body is not an integral part of human beings, Irenaeus's whole system of thought falls to pieces: the original creation is not saved, the Creator is defeated, the incarnation is not real, and his battle against the Gnostics is lost.[26]

Irenaeus's insistence on the historical and physical nature of the human animal is complemented by another insistence: that humans are made to grow into closer and closer fellowship with God. He says that "He who was the Son of God became the Son of man, that man, having been taken into the Word, and receiving the adoption, might become the son of God."[27] But Irenaeus never forgets the gap that exists between Creator and creature. He never uses the word *deification*. Instead, he uses such phrases as "to be attached to God," "to adhere to God," and "to participate in the glory of God." Although man's life is created for full fellowship with God, the line between God and us is never breached in Irenaeus's writings.[28]

We are made in the image of God. But the Word is already the true image of God. Therefore we were not only created through the Word, but in the Word. Humans are the image of the Image. In fact, the Word is only called image as incarnate: man the incarnate is the image of the incarnate God. This will become important when Irenaeus comes to discuss how in the incarnation, creation, and redemption are united, and the true image is revealed.[29]

Irenaeus states innumerable times that man is created in the image (*imago*) and similitude (*similitudo*) of God. Sharp disagreements have arisen among scholars concerning whether these are two different things or whether Irenaeus is simply repeating himself for emphasis. Irenaeus is not always careful in how he treats this issue. But the best recent scholarship has shown that they are two different things.[30] In fact, Irenaeus's whole treatment of the fall and redemption is hard to understand unless image and similitude are different. The image of God is human free will and our rationality. It is part of our nature and is never lost, no matter what else happens. It is what makes us morally responsible persons. On the other hand, similitude is that gift of God by which we grow in spiritual maturity and in closer communion with Him. This is impossible when we rely on our own powers. It can only be achieved by the Holy Spirit working within us. When we turn from God, as happened in the fall, we reject the Spirit, thus we reject our ability to "grow up" as persons. We fall into disorientation, decay, and eventually death. Although the image of God remains, the similitude of God is gone. No Holy Spirit, no similitude. No similitude, no salvation. For Irenaeus, salvation consists largely of a restoration of this similitude. Our human spirit or breath makes us alive and is temporal, but it is the Holy Spirit of God—who is poured out upon us by God through hearing His Word, the waters of Baptism, and in the bread and wine of the Lord's Supper—who turns us back to God.

As humans mature in the choice of the good, they grow increasingly similar to God's own goodness, love, and righteousness. That is, they grow into the *similitude* of God. Yet there is no evidence that Irenaeus mixes or confuses the divine Spirit and the human spirit. Rather, the Spirit is present to us, and only through this divine help can we make progress and mature into the full humanness that comes with growing into the similitude of God.[31]

Through it all, Irenaeus insists upon human free will as a necessary element in his dedicated opposition to the determinism of some of his Gnostic opponents, for whom our nature as spiritual beings determines our lot. Humans are responsible beings, capable of choosing good or evil. He never gives any indication that our free will is ever lost.[32]

The Fall

Turning away from the good, thus turning away from the Holy Spirit, is exactly what humanity did in Adam. Irenaeus understands the account in Genesis of the first sin this way: Humans were placed over all things. They were placed in the luxurious setting of the Garden of Eden. Because they were young or small, as the *Demonstration* words it, God placed certain limits on His human creatures for their own good so they might be grateful to Him and not arrogantly think of themselves as God. But the apostate angel, the great enemy of theirs, Satan, was jealous of humans and sought to turn them against their Creator. In the form of a serpent, he seduced the first humans into sin, promising that by eating the forbidden fruit they should be as God and receive immortality. However, Adam and Eve already possessed immortality, which they lost because of their disobedience.[33] Looking, as it were, in the wrong direction, we no longer perceive the greatness of God, and now consider ourselves the equal of our Creator.[34]

However, God saw the smallness of human beings and took pity on us. While the apostate (the serpent) did what he did because of malice, humans did it through carelessness. The divine wrath was focused on the evil angel, not on the human race. Our punishment is a relatively moderate one, and God promised a solution to the problem of sin through the seed (Genesis 3:15) of the woman, which was to be Jesus Christ.[35]

Some scholars have insisted that, compared to other Church fathers such as Augustine, Irenaeus has a "weak" doctrine of sin and corruption. There is some truth in this. Yet for Irenaeus the fall remains an unimaginable tragedy, one alleviated only by the direct intervention of God Himself. Repeatedly Irenaeus stresses the horrible effects of human disobedience: We are in Satan's power, the power of apostasy and transgression. Satan puts us to anything he wishes. Not only are we expelled from Eden, but we also are subject to many misfortunes. Wickedness has seized the entire race of men. We are so subject to our own lusts that we live like swine, cattle, and irrational beasts. We have come to look on our brothers as enemies, and we engage in every kind of murder and avarice, so God imposes upon us the fear of men (government). Worst of all, we are subjected to mortality—to decay and death. Finally, we cannot remake ourselves or save ourselves by our own instrumentality.[36]

The Recapitulation

The concept of recapitulation (*recapitulatio* in Latin or *anakephalaiosis* in Greek) stands at the center of the theology of Irenaeus. It is the heart and soul of his teachings. In it all the strands of his theology are brought together in one carefully woven tapestry.

A recapitulation is a summing up. It is going over the ground again. We already have noted that Irenaeus's organizing principle is not found in philosophical speculation but in literary categories. The word *recapitulation*, as he uses it, is a term taken from literature and rhetoric, where it is a concluding section of a speech that gathers together its argument in summary form or is a summary of a narrative.[37] The term "recapitulation" also evokes the Scriptural passages that speak about Christ being the Head (Latin *caput*, Greek *kephale*) of the Church, the firstborn of all creation, the firstborn of the dead, and the like.[38]

This recapitulation is applied by Irenaeus to the incarnation of Jesus Christ, who in His coming "sums up" the experience of the whole human race but this time does it right. He is the Second Adam who frees sinful humanity from the consequences of the First Adam. Irenaeus says:

> [T]he Word, who existed in the beginning with God, by whom all things were made, who was also always present with mankind, was in these last days, according to the time appointed by the Father, united to His own workmanship, inasmuch as He became a man liable to suffering, [it follows] that every objection is set aside of those who say, "If our Lord was born at that time, Christ had therefore no previous existence." For I have shown that the Son of God did not then begin to exist, being with the Father from the beginning; but when He became incarnate, and was made man, He commenced afresh [*in*

se ipso recapitulavit] the long line of human beings, and furnished us, in a brief, comprehensive manner, with salvation; so that what we had lost in Adam—namely, to be according to the image and likeness of God—that we might recover in Christ Jesus.[39]

In keeping with his literary and dramatic approach to the subject, Irenaeus uses the word *recapitulation* in much the same way we do—a summing up of a history or a dramatic presentation. For example, he describes the speech of Moses as "recapitulating" all that God has done for the children of Israel.[40]

The main theme in the recapitulation is one of being engaged in battle. Throughout His life, Jesus fights against Satan, the old enemy of humanity. But whereas Adam and Eve lost, Jesus will win. He is our champion, the one who fights on our behalf and emerges victorious for us. This theme of victorious battle is found everywhere in Irenaeus. It continually pops up in a variety of contexts, which shows that it is of great importance in his thinking. Christ struggles for humanity, defeats our enemy, and gives us the victory. He binds the strong man and takes his treasure. He conquers the serpent and destroys the power of the dragon. The captor is led by the conqueror as a captive. And "when Satan is bound, man is set free."[41]

Because of Christ's victory over our adversary, the tragic results of Satan's earlier victory in the Garden of Eden are reversed. Through Christ's obedience the old disobedience is done away with. Death is abolished, life is demonstrated, and communion between God and humans is restored. Man is now restored whole and can begin to grow again. The ultimate destiny for those who are thus revived is to be taken into communion with God, thus we are granted immortality: "For it was necessary, at first, that nature should be exhibited; then, after that, that what was mortal should be conquered and swallowed up by immortality, and the corruptible by incorruptibility, and that man should be made after the image and likeness of God, having received the knowledge of good and evil."[42]

It is crucial for Irenaeus that the one who accomplishes all of this must be both God and man. God, in Christ, became the first of the living because Adam had become the first of the dead. God, in Christ, was united with His own workmanship. Man could not reform himself or attain salvation, but the Son accomplished both of these by becoming incarnate.[43] His dedicated opposition to Gnosticism forces Irenaeus to insist categorically on the full humanity of Jesus Christ. First, if the very flesh of Adam was not assumed by Christ, but He took on another flesh, then the original Adam and his descendants would not have been saved through Christ's victory on the cross. But Christ did possess real flesh and blood. He fulfilled all the conditions of human nature. The physical creation is displayed in His body and blood in the Lord's Supper. He is truly "enfleshed." This occurred so there would be no other reality fashioned that was to be saved. Not only is this so, but God Himself would appear to be defeated if the Word took another substance and thus saved another humanity.[44] The Savior must be both God and man, the two being united together.[45]

The total identification of the Word, Christ, with those created in His own image is extremely important for Irenaeus. As humans grow and develop, so also Jesus Christ must go through every phase of human life. Thus He passed through infancy with the rest of humanity, being born of a virgin, Mary, who reversed the sin of Eve's disobedience by her own obedience. Jesus fasts in the desert to reverse Adam's eating of the forbidden fruit, and He resists temptation countering Adam's fall. Although the whole life of Jesus recapitulates that of fallen humanity, His death on a tree, countering Adam's disobedience through a tree, displays Jesus' ultimate identification with His creation. Irenaeus even insists that Jesus' death on the cross happened on the same day of the week as did Adam's sin. Irenaeus also believes that Jesus lived to be an old man. Relying on the statement in the Gospel of John (8:57) that He was "not yet fifty years old," Irenaeus concludes that Jesus was must have been at least 40 years old, which at that time made Jesus an old person. Clearly, Jesus' identification with and participation in all stages of human life is complete in Irenaeus's eyes.[46]

Clearly this identification with enfleshed humanity runs completely counter to the Gnostic separation of the Creator and the Savior. Likewise, it stands in the strongest possible opposition to any denial of the work of God with the children of Israel. The God incarnate in Jesus is the God of created nature, thus He is also the God of the Scriptures, that is, the Old Testament. Christ was predicted by the prophets under the direction of the Holy Spirit. He is the one who said to Moses, "I AM WHO I AM" (Exodus 3:14). He is the God of Noah, Abraham, and Isaac, proclaimed by the law and the prophets. Deuteronomy speaks of Jesus Christ. Jacob's ladder represents the cross. Christ is the son of both David and Abraham. Christ saved the sons of Israel as a type of His own passion, and in that passion He was contending for the fathers.[47]

Irenaeus's strong insistence on continuity between the God of the Old Testament and the Father of our Lord Jesus Christ leads him to stress, with equal vigor, that the Old Testament Law is not canceled but rather fulfilled in Christ. For example, Irenaeus observes that Jesus defeats the devil not by abandoning the Law but by using it against him. Irenaeus also consistently omits the Law from the mention of those powers that enslave us.[48] It is certainly true that we do not find here the understanding of the Law as nailed to the cross that we see in the writings of Paul and the writings of Martin Luther (for example, Ephesians 2:14–16; Colossians 2:13–14; LW 12:326 and elsewhere), but several aspects of Irenaeus's thought do suggest that there is an important shift in the place of the Law in the life of the Christian because of the work of Christ.

First, Irenaeus insists that the Law is intended for slaves. It was given when the children of Israel desired to return to the slavery of the fleshpots of Egypt. God granted them a Law that befitted their desired slave status. Yet this legal bondage only served to control human beings during the intervening period between Abraham and the incarnation. We are now gathered into the faith of Abraham, as are all the righteous. The Jews know God as Lawgiver, but we know Him as Father. Irenaeus insists that Abraham was made righteous by faith, and we, too, are to be saved "not by the much speaking of the law, but by the brevity of faith and love."[49] Irenaeus says:

> In like manner we also are justified by faith in God: for *the just shall live by faith.* Now, *not by the law is the promise of Abraham, but by faith*: for Abraham was justified by faith: and *for a righteous man the law is not made.* In like manner we also are justified not by the law, but by faith, which is witnessed to in the law and in the prophets, whom the Word of God presents to us.[50]

One might be tempted to see in the above passages even the *sola fide* of Luther. But some of Irenaeus's words ought to give us pause. It is the "just" or righteous ones who are gathered into this faith; it is faith "and love" that saves, not faith alone. Faith is that which receives the testimony of the Law and the prophets. One cannot escape the impression that "faith," for Irenaeus, is primarily a matter of belief—a belief that allows us to become empirically righteous. This impression, as we shall see, will be largely confirmed. For all of his quotations from Paul, Irenaeus seems much more at home in Matthew. Because one's theology often arises from a response to the problems of the day, it may be both narrow and unfair to try to force Irenaeus into a mold made by a substitutionary theology that was developed after him or fit him into lines of thought that would become the Lutheran couplets of Law and Gospel, sin and grace, faith and works, which miss what is central to Irenaeus's theology and his understanding of grace as God's unfolding plan, his dispensation from Creation to the Final Judgment.[51]

Salvation

Exactly what does all this mean for the believer? What is it in the person and work of the incarnate one, Jesus Christ, that brings God's salvation to individuals? Or, to put it somewhat crudely, what are the mechanics of salvation? How does the recapitulation, centering on the victorious battle, work salvation for humanity?

To summarize what has gone before: God created us in His image through His Word, who is already the image of the Father. To be in God's image means to be rational and to have free will. Adam and Eve still needed to grow into full humanity, which is communion with God, but they believed the lie of the devil, disobeyed God, and lost the similitude, or moral similarity, to God. However, they retained the image of God, that is, reason and free will. Being sinful, humans have become subject to decay and death. In His mercy, God the Creator Word became incarnate to rescue His handiwork by joining with it and identifying with it. He went through every stage of life, fighting the battle against our oppressors—sin, death, and the devil—and defeating them for our sake.

For Irenaeus, this salvation, wrought by the incarnation, is not a matter of some physical union in which God and man are somehow blended together. Nor is it a matter of paying a price to God nor even a ransom to the devil. Rather, it is revelation, pure and simple. By defeating our enemies, Jesus Christ reveals to us what God is like, what true man is like, and what man in union with God can do. Having seen these things, we are now open to the Spirit of God, through whom we can begin to grow into communion with God and realize our true human destiny.

What, then, is revealed? First, the incarnation, with its triumph over our enemies, reveals the graciousness of the Father; thus we need not distrust nor fear God. Irenaeus says:

Therefore God has been declared through the Son, who is in the Father, and has the Father in Himself—He who is, the Father bearing witness to the Son, and the Son announcing the Father.[52]

There is therefore one and the same God, the Father of our Lord, who also promised, through the prophets, that He would send His forerunner; and His salvation—that is, His Word—He caused to be made visible to all flesh, [the Word] Himself being made incarnate, that in all things their King might become manifest.[53]

Therefore the Son of the Father declares [Him] from the beginning, inasmuch as He was with the Father from the beginning. . . . And for this reason did the Word become the dispenser of the paternal grace for the benefit of men, for whom He made such great dispensations, revealing God indeed to men, but presenting man to God.[54]

For Irenaeus, the Word is primarily the instrument of revelation, showing the invisible God in a visible way in the incarnation. But the incarnation also reveals human nature, especially what that nature is with or without God.[55] Christ subdues him who had subdued us, and in so doing He exhibits the similitude of God. In the incarnation Christ recapitulates Adam, thus showing forth what Adam was meant to be—the image and similitude of God.[56]

Man now sees what he had not seen—the graciousness of God—and also sees his own possibilities in communion with God. The main point, of course, is that Christ, in His recapitulation, counters the lie of the devil that man has believed and that has kept man in slavery. The whole aim of the apostate (Satan) is to make human beings disbelievers in our own salvation and blasphemers against God. When such falseness enters the soul, it is the equivalent of impurity polluting the body. The object of the long-suffering of God is that man might acquire knowledge and learn the source of his deliverance; experience forgiveness, which makes him love God more; and know his own weakness and the power of God. Seeing that God is powerful and that in harmony with Him we may win the battle reverses the situation and makes Satan subject to us.

There is a plethora of citations in the works of Irenaeus that point to the fact that our victory, our restoration, comes through the revelation to us of the nature of God and of our own nature and our belief in that revelation.[57]

> For in no other way could we have learned the things of God, unless our Master, existing as the Word, had become man. For no other being had the power of revealing to us the things of the Father, except His own proper Word. . . . Again, we could have learned in no other way than by seeing our Teacher, and hearing His voice with our own ears, that, having become imitators of His works as well as doers of His words, we may have communion with Him, receiving increase from the perfect One, and from Him who is prior to all creation.[58]

Two things are important here: that the knowledge frees us to become imitators of Christ and that both the means and the goal of this imitation is fellowship or communion with God, which is the only way to righteousness, incorruptibility, and eternal life. Seeing what is done by the God-man, we become increasingly open to the presence of God in us. Irenaeus says: "The Word of God who dwelt in man, and became the Son of man, that He might accustom man to receive God, and God to dwell in man, according to the good pleasure of the Father."[59]

The Lord went through his trials so we could learn to love God. Being called back to communion with him, we receive participation in his incorruptibility. True life is found only in fellowship with God, which fellowship is to know and to enjoy His goodness. We see God and become immortal by this vision. This communion with God is effected by the Holy Spirit, whom we had abandoned—and thus lost the similitude of God—and who now dwells with us again when we are opened to Him by our knowledge of the work of recapitulation by Jesus Christ:

> For this cause, too, did Christ die, that the Gospel covenant being manifested and known to the whole world, might in the first place set free His slaves; and then afterwards, as I have already shown, might constitute them heirs of His property, when the Spirit possesses them by inheritance.[60]

Receiving the Spirit is what makes us spiritual men.[61]

As we grow in communion with the Holy Spirit, and simultaneously into the likeness of God, we are progressing morally. And according to Irenaeus we are *expected* to do so. There is no evidence at all in Irenaeus of anything close to the bound will of Augustine or the *sola fide* of Luther. Such a bound will would seem to Irenaeus to be thoroughly Gnostic. Our will remains free enough so, misdirected as it is, when it sees the truth in Jesus Christ, it may turn to God, be open to the Spirit, and grow in moral uprightness. In fact, our salvation depends upon this growth. Irenaeus declares:

> For one is the way leading upwards for all who see, lightened with heavenly light: but many and dark and contrary are the ways of them that see not. This way leads to the kingdom of heaven, uniting man to God: but those ways lead down to death, separating man from God. Wherefore it is needful for you and for all who care for their own salvation to make your course unswerving, firm and sure by means of faith, that you falter not, nor be retarded and detained in material desires, nor turn aside and wander from the right.[62]

Christ redeemed us so we should become a sanctified people, and He will return from heaven to pass judgment on all and to give good things to all who have kept His commandments.[63] What differentiates those under the new dispensation from the old is not that moral demands are done away with but that they are now kept freely, and not by the obedience of a slave.

According to Irenaeus, we must experience a complete reversal of our old way of living. In fact, Irenaeus specifically rejects the idea, held by Simon Magus (the Samaritan worker of magic from Acts 8), that we are saved by grace alone. Simon wrongly teaches that

> [M]en are saved through his grace, and not on account of their own righteous actions. For such deeds are not righteous in the nature of things, but by mere accident, just as those angels who made the world, have thought fit to constitute them, seeking, by means of such precepts, to bring men into bondage. On this account, he pledged himself that the world should be dissolved, and that those who are his should be freed from the rule of them who made the world.[64]

Irenaeus goes on to say that such beliefs as those of Simon Magus lead men into lives of debauchery.[65]

But the growth and progress of the Christian life, which is made possible by the victory of the Second Adam and the help of the Holy Spirit, still takes place in persons who are only gradually maturing and who live in a world that is still hostile. The roadblocks of the world will be overcome only at the end time, when Christ shall return, when recapitulation will be complete, and when the rule of God will be established. Irenaeus is well aware of the ambiguity of our present situation and places great stress on the final consummation. In fact, he devotes almost all of Book V of *Against Heresies* to the return of Christ the general resurrection and related doctrines that all converge at the point of the consummation. In the final battle, the Antichrist will arise and recapitulate all evil in himself. But he will be totally defeated by Christ. The righteous will have their bodies restored and will reign in a restored creation in which there will be harmony (even the lion will eat straw) and in which the whole creation will be liberated from the slavery of perishability and take part in the glorious liberty of the sons of God.[66]

Irenaeus and Grace

The Gnostic controversy raged for decades and reached its peak in the later part of the second century, when it almost became the dominant force in the Church, except for the Church's insistence on clinging to the witness of the whole of Scripture. After Irenaeus's death, Gnosticism tended to lose its momentum, though its central concerns and tenets have popped up throughout the history of the Christian Church, most notably in the teachings of the Manichaeans, active during the time of Augustine in the fourth and fifth centuries; the Albigenses in the High Middle Ages; and a number of "spiritual" movements in modern times. Gnosticism's deep concern for the spiritual nature of human beings has served as a constant and salutary reminder that we are more than mere physical creatures. Yet Gnosticism's insistence that our souls are of the same substance as God, that creation is evil, and that Christ was not a real man have seemed, to many, to cut at the heart of the Christian message. Irenaeus saw it this way, and it was he, along with some others, who was largely responsible for the defeat of Gnosticism, countering it with his own comprehensive understanding of the Christian faith.

It may come as a surprise and somewhat of a disappointment that Irenaeus, one of the earliest and greatest of Christian thinkers, says little or nothing about the death of Jesus Christ on the cross as payment to God or to anyone else for the sins of humanity. In fact, Irenaeus's focus was much broader. For him the whole *oikoumene*, the whole arrangement or dispensation, is grace. Both the dispensation and grace encompassed the entire range of history from creation to consummation. Both brought about the eventual restoration of all nature, centering on the salvation of humans because it is with us that ruin began. Both came to its climax in the incarnation of the Creator Word, whose work reveals to us both the love of God and what the Second Adam, a truly mature human, is like. This revelation gives us that *gnosis* that turns us again to God and opens us to His Spirit, by whose power and guidance we can again begin our growth toward maturity as human persons, eventually finding our true home in communion with God.

Irenaeus did not have a sophisticated, well worked-out doctrine of the Trinity. That would come much later, as we shall see. Yet he clearly held to a threefold understanding of God's activity, and that understanding was totally infused by grace: Creation was an act of gracious love; the incarnation was the power of God working on our behalf to free us, without our merit; and our growth in the Christian life is impossible without the work of the Holy Spirit. As Gustaf Aulen expresses:

> The whole dispensation is the work of grace. Mankind that had fallen into captivity is now by God's mercy delivered out of the power of them that held them in bondage. God had mercy upon his creation and bestowed upon them a new salvation through his Word, that is, Christ, so that men might learn by experience that they cannot attain to incorruption by themselves, but by God's grace only.[67]

Or as Irenaeus himself explains:

> [W]hile man, who had been led captive in times past, was rescued from the grasp of his possessor, according to the tender mercy of God the Father, who had compassion on His own handiwork, and gave to it salvation, restoring it by means of the Word—that is, by Christ—in order that men might learn by actual proof that he receives incorruptibility not of himself, but by the free gift of God.[68]

According to Irenaeus, it is by the grace of God that we are freed to grow into the persons that we were created to be.

Note on the Development of the Canon of Scripture and the Creeds

The origins of the specifically Christian Scriptures, the New Testament, are complex, sometimes obscure, and much debated. A full treatment of this issue is well beyond the scope of this book. However, the Gnostic and Marcionite controversies did have a hand in forcing the Church to decide which books should be included in the authoritative collection of works, the canon.

As the community struggled with this issue, the main question was often which books were acceptable to be read in worship services. Marcion, who rejected God as the Creator and Lawgiver, appropriately also rejected all the works of the Creator's people, the Jews. This meant that he tossed out the entire Hebrew Bible, what we call today the Old Testament. Even works or sections of works from the Christian community that displayed any Jewish influences, such as the Gospel of Matthew, must also be rejected, according to Marcion. This position left Marcion and his followers with a small Bible that consisted only of ten letters of Paul and Luke/Acts. Even these documents Marcion edited to eliminate "Jewish" influences.

The Gnostics, on the other hand, produced a large number of books, primarily in support of their mythologies. Therefore, their canon was a good deal larger than that of Marcion. The Gnostics not only added books to what we would now call the New Testament, but they also included some sections of the Old Testament. When they did include Old Testament material, it was always with their own interpretations, which fit with their understanding of the faith. The Gnostic tendency was often to reverse traditional interpretations. For example, they might deal with the account of creation and the fall in Genesis so the lower god, the demiurge or some other similar being, creates the world. The serpent becomes the representative of the high god, who tells Adam and Eve that they will discover their own divine nature by eating of the tree of knowledge. He is tempting them, not to sin but to true *gnosis*. The creator god resents their new knowledge, which will free them, thus the creator expels them from paradise.

The Church, as it struggled with these and other issues that impinged on the question of the canon of Scripture, found an increasing commonness concerning those books considered to be acceptable. Although there was no official council or edict that proclaimed the acceptable writings, by about AD 200 there had developed something approaching a consensus on the matter. The collection of writings the Church had at this time was the same, or nearly the same, as what we today call the New Testament.

The formulation of creeds was also common during this early period of the church.[69] It seems that each congregation or district had its own confession of faith that was connected with the Baptism ceremony. These creeds were largely in the form of questions—"Do you believe . . . ?"—to which was given the answer, "I believe . . . " Creeds were almost always threefold, following Jesus' command recorded in the Gospel of Matthew to baptize in the name of the Father, Son, and Holy Spirit.

As the theological battles of the second century were waged, creeds became insistent on affirming what the Gnostics and Marcionites rejected: the God we worship is the Creator; Jesus Christ really was born and really died; it is the body, not just the spirit, that is resurrected. The creed that is the mainstay of Western Christianity, the Apostles' Creed, is modeled on an ancient Roman baptismal formula, known as the Old Roman Symbol, which probably originated during the period of Irenaeus (the second century) or shortly thereafter. It is interesting that the Old Roman Symbol does not mention that God is the creator. Only centuries later, likely under the influence of ancient Eastern creeds, was this added to what is know known as the Apostles' Creed, a creed that affirms what the Gnostics and Marcionites denied.

2

The Trinitarian Controversy: From Nicaea to Constantinople

Introduction

I t is often the case in the Early Church that a problem is "solved," or at least resolved, to the satisfaction of a particular community or group. Although this particular community's questions are answered, new questions arise for which the solution provides no answers. Such is the case with the Trinitarian Controversy, often referred to as the Arian Controversy. The Church had emerged from the chaos of the second century stronger than ever. It had survived persecution and suffering; it had found in its Scriptures and in its episcopacy authorities on which it could rely. Perhaps most important, the Church had established once and for all that the Word had been the instrument of creation, affirming that creation is good, and that in the incarnation that Word had taken on real flesh and blood.

In the fourth century, however, a new set of questions arose for which the outcomes of the old controversies offered no answers. These questions concerned whether that Word, by whom we are saved, is really God or a creature. Does God Himself save us? This debate not only rocked and split the Church, it also threatened to divide the Roman Empire itself. For some involved in the controversy, it was about the dignity of God. For others, it concerned the very salvation of humanity.

Once the Arian Controversy began, it involved, literally, a cast of thousands. But there were many persons and ideas that gave rise to the controversy. Without some knowledge of this background, it is difficult to follow the intricacies of the struggle or to understand why so many people were so agitated about the issues. We will take a short look at one theologian (Origen), one movement (Sabellianism), and one emperor (Constantine) as means to better understand what led up to the Arian Controversy.

Origen

Quite simply, Origen (died ca. AD 251) is one of the great intellects in the history of the Christian Church. He was an outstanding teacher at Alexandria in Egypt, which by the third century had come to rival or surpass Athens as the intellectual center of the Roman Empire. Alexandria also boasted both Christian and pagan teachers of high repute.

Origen also was a man thoroughly dedicated to his faith. The story is told that as a boy he was eager to join his father as a martyr, but he was prevented from doing so by his mother, who hid his clothes. It is also reported that Origen had himself castrated so he could work with women without giving cause for scandal. His childhood wish to be a martyr for the faith was granted when he was arrested during one of the general persecutions that the Church faced. Origen died as a result of the torture he was made to suffer.

Origen considered himself a Christian Gnostic, but he insisted that enlightenment could come only as a result of prayer and the study of Scripture, to which he devoted his many talents.

Like Irenaeus, Origen saw the Christian life as a journey toward maturity. Also like Irenaeus, Origen insisted on the free will of humans. Unlike Irenaeus, Origen was given to those speculations about a higher world that Irenaeus so thoroughly rejected. Origen was much influenced by a philosophy called Middle Platonism. Indeed, he may have been one of the persons instrumental in developing its doctrines.

Plato developed a philosophy that stressed the higher, more spiritual, values. He learned from his teacher, Socrates, that wisdom consists in understanding such general truths as justice and piety and living by them. Plato developed this insight into a philosophical system that encompassed all aspects of reality, including doctrines of morality, human nature, politics, and more. The entire system depended on ascending to higher and higher truths, culminating in insights into the Good, the True, and the Beautiful.

As the centuries passed, Plato's followers took his views in an even more spiritual direction. Thus emerged the philosophy called Middle Platonism and, later, Neo-Platonism. Both of these philosophical systems considered true wisdom to be an understanding that went well beyond mere sensual, empirical knowledge. True wisdom could only be achieved through intellectual rigor, self-discipline, and moral purity.

Middle Platonism was probably *the* important philosophy of Origen's day, the finest intellectual expression of the culture of the time. As a Christian and a seeker after truth, Origen found that Middle Platonism lent itself to be the vehicle through which he could both understand and express his faith. Christian thinkers through the centuries have followed in this path, making honest use of Stoicism, Neo-Platonism, Aristotelianism, Existentialism, and other philosophical systems. Experience has shown that there are important opportunities and advantages in this approach, which may be necessary to expressing the Christian faith in understandable and teachable terms, but there are accompanying pitfalls and dangers as well.

As someone who read his Bible through Platonic eyes, Origen was never content with the literal understanding of its passages. Instead, he sought their spiritual meaning. This led him to emphasize strongly the allegorical interpretation of Scripture, an approach that would become standard for those who would follow him in the Alexandrian school. (Such an interpretative approach would be used by others as well, like Augustine of Hippo, Pope Gregory I ["the Great"], and the venerable Didymus, the last and one of the greatest teachers at the catechetical school in Alexandria that taught Jerome and many others.) Although helpful in plumbing the depths of divine mysteries, this allegorical interpretation often left itself open to the widest kind of speculation. For example, Origen understands the Gospel account of Jesus' entry into Jerusalem "mounted on a donkey, and on a colt" (Matthew 21:5) to be a reference to Law and Gospel because Jesus could not possibly be riding on two animals at once. Other allegorical interpretations include those of Augustine, who treated the steps of creation in Genesis as steps to inner enlightenment, and Pope Gregory the Great, who in his commentary on the Book of Job, known as the *Moralia*, found allegorical meanings to almost every word of Scripture.

Origen's theological system is much too profound and too aesthetically beautiful to be summed up in a few words, but for our purposes a short outline will have to suffice.[1] Origen saw all reality as a progression from unity to multiplicity and then on to unity again. Reality begins with the one God who, out of love, creates a multitude of beings through His Word. But even here a kind of unity is preserved in the harmony of all these beings as they orbit around God, basking in the warmth of His love. Sad to say, these beings eventually "cool off" in their affection, thus they fall from Him. In a sense they receive bodies as punishment for their sin, but in another way of looking at it, the solid bodies are a natural result of their cooling off.

One of these spiritual beings, the soul of Jesus, remains loyal and does not fall away. In fact it grows in affection for the Word, and unity with the Word in such a complete manner that its being is radiated by the Word, just as iron glows when thrust into the fire.[2] (The phrase "iron in the fire" will become an important part of the theological vocabulary of many of the teachers of the Church.) In the incarnation, the Word becomes incarnate in union with this soul, and the process of reunion with God is begun. It will culminate when all beings turn back to God and are eventually united with Him, and He again will be all in all.

Origen's magnificent portrayal of reality and its salvation would have a profound effect on future Christian thinkers, especially in the East. Yet for all of his brilliance, he left one basic question unanswered: He never made it clear whether he considered the Word to be fully God, as the Father was, or a subordinate divine being or even a creature, perhaps the first and best of all creatures, but a creature nonetheless. Origen could proclaim the unity of God in the strongest terms, even using the word *homoousios* ("one substance") to refer to the relation of the Father to Son.[3] This word will become the center of great controversy, as we shall see. On the other hand, Origen also could suggest that the Father and the Son are separate beings, or *hypostases*, united by harmony and will.[4] As a result of this lack of clarity, his followers divided into what has been called the "right-wing Origenists," who believe that the Word was completely divine, and the "left-wing Origenists," who saw the Word as somehow subordinated to the Father. It should be noted that "Word" theology always had a tendency to leave itself open to just such questions. The Arian Controversy was to some extent the outcome of this division within the camp of those who followed Origen.

Sabellianism

This theological movement grew up, at least in part, as a reaction to Gnosticism. The Gnostics had proclaimed a god who descended by degrees—trickled down, if you will. This was understandably offensive to those who cherished the uniqueness and unity of God. These latter folk were also suspicious of Word theology, which they also saw as asserting degrees of subordination within the divine substance—a second god. In opposition to such suspect views, they placed an extreme emphasis on the unity of God. Because of this, the sect is sometimes called "Monarchians," from *mono-arche*, the one ultimate principle.

One of the early leaders of this school of thought was Sabellius (who flourished in Rome from AD 200 to about AD 220), so his followers are sometimes called Sabellians. He and many of his fellow believers insisted so strongly on the oneness of God that they believed that Father, Son, and Holy Spirit were all identical, just different expressions or modes of the same divine reality. This subsect of the Monarchians was given the third name of Modalists because of their belief in these "modes" of divine reality. According to the Modalists, this one divine substance sometimes appeared as Father, sometimes as Son, and at other times as Holy Spirit. For example, the one who died on the cross was the same as the Father. This view caused opponents in the West to give the Modalists a fourth name, a disparaging nickname: *Patripassians*, or "Father-sufferers."

Paul of Samosata, archbishop of Antioch from AD 260–272, was evidently one of a somewhat smaller group within the Monarchian fold that bore the label "Dynamic" Monarchians. This subsect also held to the absolute unity of God, as did the Modalists, but preserved the divine unity by keeping Jesus Christ out of it. The human Jesus only received power (Greek *dunamis*) from God. The views of Paul of Samosata, like those of the Modalists, seemed to collapse the threefoldness of the Christian experience of God. The importance of Paul of Samosata for our purposes is that he was condemned by a council of bishops in AD 268. In condemning him, the council also condemned the word that was associated with his way of thinking. The outlawed Greek word was *homoousion*, or "of one substance," a word that seemed to express exactly those ideas the assembled bishops found heretical.[5] It is this word, among others, that would divide the Church for decades during the Arian Controversy.

Constantine the Great

During the second half of the third century, Christians tended to do quite well. They were becoming more accepted, there were no general persecutions, and some Christians even rose to relatively high positions in the Roman Empire. However, the empire itself was not faring all that well. It was ruled by a series of generals who seized power from other generals, one after the other. They were called the "barracks emperors." In the period from AD 235 to AD 284, about a half-century, there were twenty-six emperors, of whom twenty-five died violent deaths. Something would have to be done to ensure the stability of the empire.

The last in this series of barracks emperors was Diocletian. He was astute enough to see that Rome's administrative structure needed serious overhaul. The empire was too big and unwieldy, he believed, so he divided it in two: the Eastern and Western Empires, each with an Augustus to rule it. Second, he solved the problem of succession by having each Augustus appoint a Caesar as second in command. This Caesar would succeed him at his death. Diocletian's careful administrative plans would soon come unraveled, however, as we shall see.

Diocletian also persecuted Christians, blaming the hard times in the empire on those of alien spirit. The story is told that he had ordered the pagan priests to perform an act of augury or divination known as *haruspices*, an Etruscan cultic act that had become widely popular in the empire by Jesus' lifetime. In this act, a soothsayer or *haruspex* cut open animals in a ceremony that involved examining the entrails to predict future events. The procedure failed repeatedly, so the emperor looked for a foreign presence that might be disturbing the proper atmosphere. Because

Christians were present, his wrath fell on them. The persecution of Christians under Diocletian, which began in earnest in AD 303 at the instigation of his subordinate Galerius, was more thoroughgoing and more vicious than any previously experienced. Maximian, the father of Constantine's rival Maxentius, added to this persecution, which grew in strength and lasted in various edicts until 308–310, when the fortunes of several leaders changed.

The unfortunate result of Diocletian's well-laid plans was that upon his forced retirement, together with Maximian, he left the empire with four rulers, Constantius and Galerius, with their two successors, Severus and Maximinus, Galerius's toadies. Each was tempted to gain power at the expense of the others. Added to this, a number of generals were lurking just behind the scenes, eager to assume the royal purple. Thus following Diocletian's retirement in AD 305 (he died in either 313 or 316), chaos reigned. By AD 312, after the death, suicide, or military defeat of various rulers, it came down to four men competing for the rule of the empire. In the East, Maximinus, the most ardent persecutor of Christians following Galerius, faced off against Licinius. In the West, Maxentius, who had been an ardent persecutor of Christians like his father until about AD 310, opposed Constantine.

Constantine's father had been a general in Britain. Upon his father's death in AD 306, Constantine assumed command of his father's troops, who in turn proclaimed Constantine "Augustus." He headed cautiously for Rome, solidifying his territory, and eventually prepared to do battle with Maxentius after years of preparation and conquest. Thus the stage was set for one of the most crucial battles in the history of the Church and indeed in the history of the Western World.

Constantine (died AD 337) had always been more favorably disposed to Christians than the others vying for the leadership of Rome. He even had a Spanish bishop, Hosius of Cordova, as one of his chief advisors. But Constantine's relation to the Church was solidified by the outcome of the battle. According to Constantine's own account, before the battle, he saw the letters *chi rho*—the first letters of the name *Christ* in Greek—superimposed on each other in the sky. The letters were surrounded by the words "In this sign conquer."[6] Constantine ordered his troops to bear this "sign of Constantine" into combat, and at the battle of Mulvian Bridge in October of AD 312, he won! Thus the Western Empire of Rome was now headed by a man who not only was sympathetic to the Christian faith, but also one who felt he owed his crown to the Christian God.

Constantine was not slow in showing his gratitude. Early in AD 313, he met with Licinius to issue the Edict of Milan, granting toleration to all religions but singling out Christians for special protection. Around that time, Licinius defeated Maximinus. The field of rivals narrowed to two, but there could only be one. Eventually Constantine defeated Licinius and became the sole ruler of the Roman Empire, a position he was able to maintain. Constantine gave money to some Christian churches and built others. He granted the clergy special privileges. He promulgated laws favoring Christianity, including Sabbath laws. Perhaps most significant, Constantine moved his capital from Rome, which was full of pagan temples, to the city of Byzantium, which would be a new Rome, a Christian Rome, a city filled with churches. It would now be called, understandably, Constantinople.

Constantine never "established" Christianity—that is, made it the official religion of the Roman Empire. That would come later. But he did everything else to favor it. Scholars debate whether he was sincere in all his efforts on behalf of the Christians. Some believe he was using the Christian faith as a kind of spiritual glue to hold together a sagging empire. Whatever his motives, Constantine surely began the development of a relationship between church and state, a relationship that would prove important in European history. Of course Constantine was just as eager to control the Christian Church as to support it.

Constantine brought about a total reversal of the situation for Christians. Immediately prior to his rise to the emperor's throne, Christians had been persecuted outcasts. Now they were favored citizens. Believers reacted in various ways to the work of Constantine. It is certainly understandable that many considered him to be a kind of secular savior, sent by God to relieve them of their previous painful plight. Others were skeptical, fearing that the holy Church was now in bed with the empire that had been a symbol of demonic evil. But one thing was certain, everything was now new. The Church was stepping onto uncharted ground with little from the past to guide it. Just as when Christianity left its Jewish cradle to walk in the Hellenistic world, so now it would have to adjust to a radically new cultural situation, not only in practice but also in its theology. It was inevitable that new conditions would call forth new understandings of the Christian faith and practice.

The three strands we have just discussed—the theology of Origen, with its lack of clarity about the status of the Word; the fear of Modalism and the accompanying condemnation of *homoousion*; and the new situation for the Christian Church under Constantine—all converged, with other forces to be sure, to present the Church with its second great crisis: the Trinitarian Controversy.

Arius and Alexander

In the year AD 323, Patriarch Alexander of Alexandria issued an official condemnation of Arius, one of his clergy, accusing him of heresy—corrupting the true faith.[7] From the charges made (the bill of particulars), we can glean the main concern of Alexander concerning his wayward subordinate: Arius was dedicated to the absolute perfection of God, His utter transcendence and unchangeability. This stood at the center of Arius's piety.[8] According to Arius, God could never be altered in any way, or He would no longer be God.

There were probably several sources of the views Arius held. One, of course, was the biblical understanding of the greatness, the holiness, and the transcendence of the God of Israel, who existed far beyond what mere humans could understand. Another source may well come from Aristotle, whose philosophy Arius clearly favored. Aristotle, you may recall, saw God as that perfection toward which all reality was drawn. Yet God was not drawn to any reality, imperfect as it was, because this would draw Him to what was imperfect; thus He would be lowered. If we may put it this way, Aristotle's god is like a beautiful woman whose beauty attracts and sets in motion a number of men, but this woman is blissfully unaware of the men and unaffected by them. The god of Aristotle, in a manner similar to the hypothetical woman, remains uninvolved and undisturbed by the world. He is the Unmoved Mover or the Self-thinking Thought. This philosophy or something close to it was likely behind Arius's teachings.

Arius believed, as did almost all Christians by this point in the fourth century, that God created through the Word and that this Word was incarnate in Jesus Christ. But if this is true, Arius reasoned, then the Word is involved in the changes that come with creation. Even more, this Word was definitely subject to change as He walked the earth, hungered, cried, grew up, and suffered. However, these changes could not be true of God. The conclusion Arius reached was that the Word through whom all was created and who became incarnate for us was not God.

All of Arius's statements, which were listed by Archbishop Alexander when he deposed him, support his main concern with saving the high God from imperfection and change. Thus Arius insisted that the Word was not of the divine nature but a creature—perhaps the first and best of all creatures, but a creature still. Arius also taught that the Word was not eternal but, unlike the eternal Father, the Word had a beginning. Thus the Father was not always Father because there was not always a Son. Further, according to Arius the Word was not from the divine substance but was created out of nothing. Being a creature, the Word is actually unlike the god of Arius, foreign to his essence, and subject to change as all creatures are. Theoretically, says Arius, the Word might even change for the worse as the devil did. For Arius, the Word was a mediator, standing between his god and human beings without being either. It appears that, like Aristotle, Arius cannot abide the notion that the unchanging God and changeable matter can be united. In a way somewhat reminiscent of the Gnostics, God and the world are held apart, yet in this case it is to preserve a god that conforms to "what a god should be."

It was these views that Archbishop Alexander believed challenged the heart of the Christian faith, which strongly affirmed that in the incarnation it was God Himself who saves us. With Alexander's formal deposing of Arius, the battle was joined, and partisans gathered on both sides. The entire Eastern portion of both church and empire became inflamed over the issue, and both institutions were in danger of being split. Whatever else motivated Constantine, he at least had some understanding that the Christian faith held together his realms. He wrote to both sides, telling them to cool down. He was clearly nonplused that what he considered a mere theological debate should so threaten the stability of the empire. The emperor evidently wanted his realm to be moderate, including all, Christian and pagan, who subscribed to some kind of general monotheism. What he could not abide was anything he considered to be a disruptive and stubborn religious extremism. This would become clear enough as the controversy raged on.[9] Constantine's pleas did no good; the battle continued onward.

Constantine refused to be thwarted in this matter, so he called a church council. The representatives would meet at Nicaea, near Constantinople, to decide the matter. This would be the first of the seven great ecumenical councils that tackled one controversy after another for more than 500 years, the last being held in AD 787.

The Council of Nicaea

Many aspects of the Council of Nicaea are disputed because no records appear to have been kept. However, scholars have gleaned an understanding of the events from a number of sources.[10] Thus we know that in the summer of AD 325, the 218 Fathers of Nicaea assembled for the council (though the exact number of bishops is unknown). Almost all these bishops were from the East, but the pope (the head of the Western church and stationed in Rome) sent representatives. Constantine was present at the council, though he was not a bishop or even a baptized Christian. His advisor, Hosius, chaired the meetings.

Early in the proceedings, the Arians presented a statement of their beliefs, which was quickly condemned by the vast majority of those present at the council. The assembly then attempted to reach an agreement on what the Church affirmed and what it condemned. This was not easy. Although almost all the bishops had creeds developed for their own areas, these statements of belief were almost useless for the present debate because they dealt with issues from the past and said little or nothing that pertained to the present controversy with the Arians. Old formulas did not cover new challenges. Further, when the body attempted to find terms or biblical citations that would eliminate Arianism, the Arians repeatedly managed to interpret the passages in ways that appeared supportive to their positions.

According to the reports of the church historian Eusebius, Constantine stepped into the fray and made the momentous suggestion that the word *homoousios* be inserted into the statement of belief being developed by the council. It is not exactly clear why the emperor made this suggestion or from whom he had received it.[11] One thing was readily apparent: It was the one word that the Arians could not abide. The council adopted the suggestion.

The final decree of Nicaea, including added condemnations, tries to eliminate in every way possible any suggestion of Arianism from the Christian faith. It reads as follows:

We believe in one God, the Father almighty, maker of all things visible and invisible;

And in one Lord Jesus Christ, the Son of God, begotten from the Father, only-begotten, that is, from the substance [*ousia*] of the Father, God from God, light from light, true God from true God, begotten not made, of one substance [*homoousion*] with the Father, through Whom all things came into being, things in heaven and things on earth, Who because of us men and because of our salvation came down and became incarnate, becoming man, suffered and rose again on the third day, ascended to the heavens, and will come to judge the living and the dead;

And in the Holy Spirit.

But as for those who say, There was when He was not, and, Before being born He was not, and that He came into existence out of nothing, or who assert that the Son of God is of a different hypostasis or substance, or is created, or is subject to alteration or change—these the Catholic Church anathematizes.[12]

Almost all those present at the Council of Nicaea signed the final document. Arius and some of his most loyal followers refused and were condemned by the council. Constantine sent them into exile. The handwriting was on the wall for the future.

After Nicaea

The matter of the Arian Controversy was settled after the Council of Nicaea, or so it appeared. Those who clung to the full divinity of the Word were victorious, the Arians were routed, and the controversy was resolved. In fact, however, the fuse had merely been lit for further explosions. Nicaea was only the first round in a prolonged and difficult fight. First, Constantine would change sides in the debate. He came under the influence of Eusebius of Nicomedia, a devout Arian, and increasingly leaned to their side. Eventually Constantine recalled the exiles, though Arius died during his triumphal return. Eusebius of Nicomedia took over the leadership of the movement upon Arius's death. Constantine now persecuted the Nicaeans in a manner similar to the former treatment of the Arians. He was baptized on his death bed AD 337 by Eusebius the Arian. His son Constantius then ruled in the East. He followed his father's footsteps by continuing to persecute the Nicaean party.

The theological situation was even more alarming for the Nicaeans because a whole spectrum of positions concerning the Godhead competed for allegiance. Those opposed to the outcome of the Council of Nicaea divided roughly into three main parties. On one end were the Arians, small in numbers but dedicated and often given imperial backing. The Arians tried desperately to make all others see the logic and apparent biblical basis of their position. A second group, the largest, consisted of bishops who were far from being Arians but who could not stomach the word *homoousios*. They considered it to be Sabellian, so they resisted any acceptance of the Nicaean formula (creed). The third group, which overlapped with the second, would put forth moderate options to *homoousious*.[13]

All these groups either opposed or considered with great hesitation the Council of Nicaea and its dedicated defenders, whose main spokesman was Athanasius.

Athanasius

Athanasius had served as Alexander of Alexandria's secretary at the Council of Nicaea. Upon Alexander's death in AD 328, Athanasius succeeded as archbishop or patriarch of Alexandria. Athanasius was one of those rare individuals who sticks to his guns no matter what. He maintained "firmness in the right as God gave him to see the right." Saintly and stubborn, Athanasius devoted his life to the defense of the Council of Nicaea. For his troubles, he was condemned repeatedly by his fellow clergy. He was exiled five times by various emperors. His major works relevant to our discussion are *The Incarnation of the Word* and the *Four Discourses against the Arians.*[14]

Athanasius and Arius were diametrically opposed. Arius, as we have seen, found his starting place for his theology in the perfection of God, from which all else followed. Athanasius's starting point was salvation. His choice of starting points was not the result of philosophical reasonings but was a deeply felt and all-consuming passion for the salvation of the human soul.

According to Athanasius, the need for a radical solution to our human condition of sin was necessitated by our fall from the created state. In the beginning, God, through His Word, made humans out of nothing. Being so created, we have the tendency to return to nonbeing. So we could continue in communion with God in blessedness and immortality and not return to nothing, He made us in His own image. That is, God made us rational. By turning away from God, we lost our knowledge of Him, rejected grace, and returned to our natural state of mortality.

Athanasius averred that God has made it possible for us to know Him through nature and through the Law and the prophets; however, being devoid of reason, we have turned to lawlessness. According to Athanasius, the overall effects of the fall are devastating:

> For . . . man sinned and is fallen, and by his fall all things are in confusion; death prevailed from Adam to Moses (cf. Rom v. 14), the earth was cursed, Hades was opened, Paradise shut, heaven offended, man, lastly, corrupted and brutalised (cf. Ps. xlix. 12), while the devil was exulting against us.[15]

By far the most dire result of human rebellion was the destruction of our relationship with God. It brought with it corruption, dissolution, and that ultimate corruption, death:

> [B]ut men . . . received the condemnation of death with which they had been threatened; and from thenceforth no longer remained as they were made, but were being corrupted according to their devices; and death had the mastery over them as king. For transgression of the commandment was turning them back to their natural state, so that just as they have had their being out of nothing, so also, as might be expected, they might look for corruption into nothing in the course of time.[16]

According to Athanasius, the human problem is just this corruptibility. Salvation consists in the restoration of our union with God, which includes the restoration of eternal life. Beings in decay and death could only be restored by union with Him who is Life and Immortality. When we become so permeated by the divine presence, like iron in the fire, we become "deified." In one of his most quoted phrases, Athanasius says, "For He was made man that we might be made God."[17] As a result, we, like God, can overcome corruption and death and become immortal.

The ultimate expression of the Word's identification with us is His death. Athanasius sees this event as a sacrifice, a ransom paid to the Father. It is the payment of a debt owed—the debt of death. God cannot leave to destruction the race in which He has planted His image. Yet neither can He ignore the rebellion and its necessary outcome. What was God to do? Only His own Word was worthy to suffer on behalf of all: "For being Word of the Father, and above all, He alone of natural fitness was both able to recreate everything, and worthy to suffer on behalf of all and to be the ambassador for all with the Father."[18]

More important, the immortal Word took to Himself a mortal body. Flesh, of course, could die, but the Word could not. Thus at the crucifixion the body did die, but the Word remained alive and incorruptible. By the death of the body, He abolished death in Himself. The dead body was again permeated with His life.[19] Christ showed by the resurrection that He was more powerful than death and that He could make His own body incorruptible, the firstfruits of our resurrection. God had delivered man to Him

> [I]n order that He might be made man, and all things be renewed in him. For man, being in Him, was quickened: for this was why the Word was united to man, namely, that against man the curse might no longer prevail . . . that both the judgment of death which hung over us may be delivered to the Son, and that he may then, by dying for us, abolish it for us in Himself.[20]

The results of this life-giving union with God are just as wonderful and far-reaching as the outcome of the fall was disastrous: "All things were set right and perfected. Earth receives blessing instead of a curse, Paradise was opened to the robber, Hades cowered, the tombs were opened and the dead raised, the gates of Heaven were lifted up to await Him."[21]

According to Athanasius, we are in no way able to heal our self-inflicted wound of sin. Only God can do it, and He has done it through the incarnation of the Word. By taking on Himself human flesh, the Word has begun the process of reunion, and by His sacrificial death on the cross He has paid the price of death that we all owe to the Father. It is utterly inconceivable to Athanasius that anyone but God Himself could accomplish this, which is why he absolutely insisted that the Word is true God. Athanasius could abide nothing less. Precisely here is the heart of his disagreement with Arius. Our very salvation was at stake.

Arius, we may recall, insisted that the Word is only a creature. Athanasius, for his part, asks the following questions: "If it was to join us to God, what help is a creature?" and "What grace did he receive who was the giver of grace?"[22] The disagreement often centered on grace. Again, Arius maintained that the Word, being a creature, needed God's grace to do His work. Athanasius, on the other hand, insisted that because only God can save us, the Word must *be* God, and He is the dispenser of this grace. It is we, not the Word, that need grace. "If the Son be a creature . . . no help will come to creatures from a creature, since all need grace from God."[23] Further, and this goes to the heart of Athanasius's thinking, a creature would be changeable, so if the Word is a creature, then our salvation is unsure and the teaching about a savior-creature blasphemous.[24]

Grace and the giving of the Holy Spirit are closely connected in Athanasius, as they are in most of the writings of the Early Church fathers. Arius, as we might suspect, insisted that the Spirit was bestowed on the Son, who is a son only by participation. The response: But of what does the Son partake? Athanasius's answer: "Of the Spirit? No! But the Spirit himself partakes of the Son."[25] Again, Athanasius says:

> He had poured the Spirit on us; now to give the Spirit
> with authority is not in the power of a creature or work,
> but the Spirit is God's gift. For the creatures are hallowed
> by the Holy Spirit; but the Son, in that He is not hal-
> lowed by the Spirit, but on the contrary, Himself the
> giver of it to all, is therefore no creature but true Son of
> the Father.[26]

All of Athanasius's theology turns on the Word's coessentiality with the Father. Only when this is firmly established can our deification be assured—"that we might be made God." This kind of talk seems to suggest that Athanasius blurred the distinction between the human and the divine, the creature and the Creator. There was always a tendency among Alexandrians to come dangerously close to this pitfall, as we shall see in the next chapter.

But Athanasius, who took second place to none in stressing our union with God (that the divine permeates us), was nevertheless well aware of this danger and went out of his way to deny that this was his meaning. Indeed, it was important for him to preserve the divine/human, Savior/saved distinction, lest he fall into the same Arianism that he so abhorred. The Arians, we may recall, believed that a creature secures our salvation.

But for Athanasius the Word is God and always remains God even in the incarnation. There Christ remained impassible; He did not change in taking flesh but was only robed in it. He remained what He was.[27] For our part, though we receive the grace of the Spirit and are called sons, we are still creatures and works of nature.[28] The Son will always be a different nature from us. Unlike the Arians, who believe that we are of the same nature as the Son, Athanasius taught that our sonship is only by grace and that "thou art a man, and not God. . . . Neither we shall ever be as he, nor is the Word as we."[29] Athanasius says:

> We too become sons, not as He in nature and truth, but according to the grace of Him that calleth, and though we are men from the earth, are yet called gods, not as the True God or His Word, but as has pleased God who has given us that grace; so also, as God do we become merciful, not by being made equal to God, nor becoming in nature and truth benefactors (for it is not our gift to benefit but belongs to God), but in order that what has accrued to us from God Himself by grace, these things we may impart to others.[30]

Athanasius also had to defend himself from Arian attacks, particularly concerning his approach to Scripture. They could point to a whole host of biblical citations that supported their case, assuming, as both sides did, that the Word was the core of the person of Jesus Christ. One passage after another came to the aid of the Arians: Jesus was born; He grew up; He hungered and thirsted; He cried; He died. See, for example, Luke 2:1–7, 40–52; Matthew 4:2; John 4:6–7, 11:35, 19:28; Matthew 27:50; Mark 15:37; Luke 23:46; John 19:30. All these clearly implied suffering and change. Because God cannot change, therefore the Word cannot be God, according to the Arians.

The Arians also brought up another point that bothered them, and some non-Arians as well—that *homoousios* is never found in Scripture. Athanasius struck back. He insisted that though the word is not scriptural, its meaning is clearly biblical. Furthermore, according to Athanasius, the Arians had a distorted view of the Bible itself. They mustered piles of proof-texts to support their case, just as the Pharisees did, but missed the main message of Scripture. By fixing their gaze on the individual trees, they could not see the forest.[31]

Athanasius also attempted to throw some of the arguments of the Arians back at them. If it was logical that God needed a mediator between Himself and the world, then why not a second mediator between Him and the changeable Word, and another between Him and the second mediator, and so on? The Arians are left with an infinite regression.[32] Athanasius identified a second problem: If God needed to create a second being, the Word, to make the world, then this shows His weakness, not His strength. Because the Word is God's reason, any separation of that Word from God would leave us with an irrational God. Despite themselves, the Arians have given us a weak and lesser God, not a perfect one.[33] Third, Athanasius pointed out that once you introduce a lower heavenly being that represents God, why not more of them? Therefore, at heart the Arians are polytheists, according to Athanasius.[34]

But Athanasius's main response to his opponents came from his most deeply held belief: that the Word, our Savior, Jesus Christ, is completely divine. The toughest problems that Athanasius faced were the biblical citations that demonstrated the incarnate Word was subject to change. His reply, which he repeated over and over again, was that all those passages refer to the human Jesus that was taken up by the Word. Certainly Jesus grew up, hungered, thirsted, suffered, and the like. But the Word itself never changed. It remained as it always was—perfect and totally immune to decay and death. Otherwise, it was not God Himself who united with us, so we are not saved.[35]

Further Complications

There obviously were important issues involved in these debates, issues of central importance to all those involved. Mixed in with these issues were problems concerning the meaning of words. Sometimes different individuals use different words to mean the same thing. Then because the words are different, the individuals become convinced the meaning is different. Conversely, individuals can use the same word to mean different things. Then because the word is the same, they assume the meanings are the same. Both realities were true in the Arian Controversy and only served to complicate an already hopelessly confused situation. To better grasp the developments of the controversy, we will look at the vocabularies involved.

Tertullian (d. AD 225), one of the great thinkers of the Western Christian Church, wrote in Latin. He developed terms to express belief in the Trinity, for example, he was the first to use the word *trinitas*. Tertullian's simple formulae concerning the Trinity were influential in the Western Church. He said that though God is three [persons], He is one in substance [*una substantia*].[36] The word *sub* means "under," and the word *stantia* means "what stands." Thus the term *una substantia* literally means "that which stands under," or the basic reality behind the appearance. This "one substance" is similar to the word *homoousion* of the Council of Nicaea, which is comprised of the Greek words *homo*, which means "same," and *ousia*, which means "substance."

We have met Tertullian before. He rejected the philosophizing of Justin Martyr and others. He was also, along with Irenaeus, opposed to the Gnostics and Marcionites. But his character and other activities deserve additional mention. Tertullian was able to think clearly enough to reduce difficult concepts to precise formulations, but he also could be utterly vicious in his attacks on his opponents. Furthermore, Tertullian associated himself with a group of Christians known as Montanists. This group proclaimed that certain people among its members were ecstatic prophets, inspired by the Holy Spirit, who revealed to them truths that went beyond Scripture. Some of these messages included warnings of the coming end of the world and the need for moral rigor. In fact, a strict legalism is one of the most notable marks of the Montanists. They may be compared, not entirely unfairly, with some of the "heavenly prophets" of Luther's day, whom the reformer called "deceitful" and "mad".[37] Luther remarked that these so-called prophets, particularly one of their leaders, Doctor Andreas Bodenstein von Karlstadt, had, "devoured the Holy Spirit feathers and all."[38] Eventually the Church condemned the Montanists, and Tertullian with them. Although there were several reasons why the Montanists were rejected by the Church, one rationale was the rising institutionalization of the Christian community as it settled down for the long haul. Institutional leaders do not like "loose cannons" who may upset the balance of the larger group. Of primary importance in the rejection of the Montanists was the fear that legitimization of the group might result in almost anything being proclaimed as the will of God.

According to Early Church sources, there does not appear to be much debate about the divinity of the Holy Spirit early in the Church's existence. Eventually, however, the question of the divinity of the Word caused the parallel question of the divinity of the Holy Spirit to grow in importance. Despite Tertullian's formulae concerning the Trinity, questions surrounding the Holy Spirit gained ground during the Arian Controversy. Basil of Caesarea, to whom we will later return, would address this issue in his writings.

Although the Western formulas concerning the Trinity came from Tertullian, the Westerners, particularly at Rome, found little problem with *homoousion* as the equivalent of *una substantia*. They were the strongest supporters of the Council of Nicaea. In fact, Athanasius took refuge in Rome during one of his exiles.

Initially Athanasius did not often use *homoousion*, but the word became increasingly important to him as a test of Nicaean orthodoxy.

In the East, even supporters of the Nicaean formula, such as Hosius of Cordova (who came from Spain, a part of the Western church), tended to shy away from the controversial word *homoousion*. They used *hypostasis* instead, a word that had also been included in the Nicaean formula. This word (comprised of the Greek words *hypo*, which means "under," and *stasis*, which means "stand") is a literal rendering of the Latin *substantia*. Therefore, it could serve as well as *homoousion* as an equivalent. But as one may already suspect, the matter is more complicated. *Hypostasis* can also be understood as the reality that underlies the outer appearance of each of us—our inner selves or personality. Unfortunately, when those taking the middle position in the Arian Controversy heard this word, they became immediately suspicious that its users were asserting that there was one person in God, which meant Sabellianism was raising its ugly head.

The Way to a Solution[39]

The situation seemed hopeless. It appeared there was no way out of this thicket of politics, theology, and terminology. But things were beginning to turn on all three fronts.

The Arians started the ball rolling by proclaiming their faith in its most naked form. Some of them even used the word *anomios*, or "unlike," to refer to the Son with respect to the Father and their existence in the Godhead. Amid the many councils being held on all sides, each developing their own proclamations and creeds, the Arians managed to control one council held at Sirmium in AD 357. With imperial support, the Arians felt free to state their beliefs openly: The use of *homoousion* was banned. *Homoiousion*, which means "of like substance"—note that *homoiousion* adds the letter *i* (the Greek *iota*) to *homoousion*, which does make an iota of difference!—was also forbidden. Later, the use of *hypostasis* was also banned. *Anomios*, however, was not forbidden. Thus it was tacitly allowed. This shocked and offended many who had previously held some sympathy for the Arians. It became known as the "blasphemy" of Sirmium.

Those who had held the middle ground in the debates, who were primarily not Arians but who feared the use of *homoousion*, were also dismayed. They were shocked to see how utterly different Arianism was from what they held to be the true Christian faith. Now they were ready to move in the direction Athanasius advocated. They rallied to the word *homoiousion*, or "of like substance."

By AD 358, Athanasius was now open to compromise. He allowed the term *homoiousion*, as long as it was understood in a Nicaean sense. The old warrior died in AD 373, but new voices would arise to lead the theological battles.

The Cappadocians

Known collectively as the Cappadocians, Basil of Caesarea, his younger brother Gregory of Nyssa, and Gregory of Nazianzus were devout and brilliant Christian thinkers who were active in the Roman province of Cappadocia in Asia Minor (located in present-day Turkey). These men were able to find helpful approaches to the problems of the Trinity that were disrupting the Church. Like a growing number of bishops in the post-Constantinian empire, they were from the upper crust of society. They had received the best classical education available and could hold their own in the rough and tumble world of imperial politics, something increasingly required of bishops who were becoming burdened with matters of state as well as of Church.

Theologically and philosophically the Cappadocians were dedicated followers of Origen and his Platonic understanding of reality, but they also took for granted the correctness of the Nicaean formula. According to Plato, there was a distinction between the nature or essence of a thing and the particular expression of that essence. For example, every human being has something in common with every other human being, that is, they all share in "humanness" or human nature. But each individual is his or her own expression of that nature. By making use of this Platonic distinction between the general nature and its particular expression, Basil and Gregory of Nyssa made theological distinctions that enabled the agreement of the vast number of Christian bishops concerning the nature of the Trinity. Basil and Gregory carefully distinguished *ousia*, which they used to mean the divine reality or substance—hence *homoousion*—from *hypostasis*, which they understood as the particular persons of the Trinity. Thus they could affirm the three persons, or *hypostases*, which are all of one divine reality, or *ousia*. Their work helped to break the theological deadlock and opened the door to progress.[40]

Although all this may seem abstract, we should note that the stance taken by the Cappadocians enabled them to approach these knotty problems from the perspective of a Christian experience that begins not with a general concept of God but with the experience of a threefold grace: We exist. We have done nothing to merit it. It is a free gift. Through God's love expressed in Jesus Christ, we are forgiven. Forgiveness, too, is a gift. By the Spirit we are changed and empowered. This, too, comes freely from God. For the Cappadocians, the doctrine of the Trinity is thoroughly an affirmation of grace.

Things were also tipping the Nicaean way in politics. The Visigoths (a barbarian tribe) had been pushed to the borders of the Roman Empire by the expanding Huns in Central Asia. Mistreatment by emperors sympathetic to the Arians helped cause the Visigoths to cross the Danube and pillage the area northwest of Constantinople. During the battle of Adrianople in 378, the Arian Emperor Valens was defeated and killed, ironically by Visigoths that had converted to Arian Christianity by the missionary bishop Ulfilas. He was the first Roman emperor to be killed by barbarians on Roman soil. The handwriting was on the wall for the future of the empire, both in terms of religion and of political stability. The skilled general Theodosius I, a supporter of orthodoxy, was appointed emperor of the East to take his place. Eventually Theodosius became ruler of the entire empire, but he was the last man to rule over a united Roman Empire.

The First Council of Constantinople

Theodosius was a devout man who would later make Christianity the official religion of the Roman Empire. First, however, he intended to make all Christians orthodox, which for him meant to be in agreement with Rome. With the pieces of the puzzle beginning to come together in the matter of the Arian Controversy, he summoned a council of bishops to meet in Constantinople in AD 381. Scholars now recognize this assembly as the Second Ecumenical Council.

Although many other items found a place on its agenda, the main purpose of the council was to settle the Arian Controversy. The assembled bishops evidently took an existing creed, perhaps that of the city of Constantinople, and added to it those phrases that would ensure that it was a reaffirmation of the formula developed at Nicaea. The Second Ecumenical Council also dealt with the question of the divinity of the Holy Spirit. It had been Athanasius who again took the lead in defending this belief for reasons very similar to his defense of the *homoousion* of the Word.[41] The Cappadocians, too, insisted on the divinity of the Spirit.[42] Ambrose of Milan and others of influence also joined in.

According to scholars, Gregory of Nazianzus originally chaired the council and presided over the discussion leading up to the acceptance of its creed. However, when the bishops took to wrangling over what Gregory of Nazianzus considered to be petty ecclesiastical matters, he quit both as chair of the council and as Patriarch of Constantinople. Among other issues, the complaint was raised that Gregory was already the bishop of Nazianzus and, according to the canons of the Church, could not be a bishop of two districts.

The creed itself has become standard in both Eastern and Western Christiandom. It is usually referred to as the Nicene Creed, but it is more properly called the Niceno-Constantinopolitan Creed. It reads as follows:

> We believe in one God the Father almighty, maker of heaven and earth, of all things visible and invisible;
>
> And in one Lord Jesus Christ, the only-begotten Son of God, begotten from the Father before all ages, light from light, true God from true God, begotten not made, of one substance with the Father [*homoousion to patri*], through Whom all things came into existence, Who because of us men and because of our salvation came down from heaven, and was incarnate from the Holy Spirit and the Virgin Mary and became man, and was crucified for us under Pontius Pilate, and suffered and was buried, and rose again on the third day according to the Scriptures and ascended to heaven, and sits on the right hand of the Father, and will come again with glory to judge living and dead, of Whose kingdom there will be no end;
>
> And in the Holy Spirit, the Lord and life-giver, Who proceeds from the Father, Who with the Father and the Son is together worshipped and together glorified, Who spoke through the prophets; in one holy Catholic and apostolic Church. We confess one baptism to the remission of sins; we look forward to the resurrection of the dead and the life of the world to come. Amen.[43]

One important note: Westerners who use this creed in worship services will observe that the original creed speaks only of the procession of the Spirit from the Father. The phrase "and the Son" (*filioque*) was added later in the West, based on the writings of

Augustine of Hippo, formulated in Spain about 589 to reject Arianism and Sabellianism and championed by Charlemagne as King of the Franks and Holy Roman Emperor (AD 800–814). The Eastern Orthodox Church has never accepted this addition. Their objections are twofold. First, they insist that no one should dare to make additions to the decrees of an ecumenical council, which they consider sacred. Second, the phrase is objectionable on theological grounds. They prefer the phrase "from the Father, through the Son" formulated by Gregory of Nyssa.[44] The addition of this phrase is one thing that still divides the Eastern and Western churches.

The First Council of Constantinople struck the death knell for Arianism as an organized force within the Christian Church. But as these things usually go, the war was not completely over. Vestiges of Arianism remained. In particular, the barbarians who were to serve as both invaders and as members of the Roman army were often Arians. They had been converted by Arian missionaries and brought their beliefs with them into the empire. Yet Arianism would never again threaten to be a mainstream force within Christianity. The Council of Constantinople firmly established that it is God who saves us. The doctrine of the Trinity was and remains the major expression of that faith.

3

The Christological Controversy

To put the matter somewhat simplistically, the outgrowth of the Gnostic Controversy had been the affirmation that Jesus was truly human. In addition to defining the Trinity, the Arian Controversy, resulted in the Church's affirmation that the Word in Christ was truly divine. Now the question arises: What is the relation between that human and that divine in Jesus Christ? Here, as previously, we will encounter a veritable parade of theologies, councils, individual and corporate egos, and imperial interference that will split the Church in ways that have not been entirely resolved to this day.

This may seem to be one of the more "picky" issues to arise as the Church attempted to understand its own basic beliefs, particularly because it caused so much division and grief. But perhaps its importance can be highlighted by looking at it in terms of how we believe that God acts in every believer—*in each of us*. Because Jesus is the New Adam, the "firstborn among many brothers" (Romans 8:29), He is believed to open the door to all of us to experience in some way a similar kind of relation to the

Father that He has. So in this debate, we are not only raising questions about who Jesus is, but about ourselves as well. "What is Jesus' relation to the Father?" and "What is our relation to the Father?" are closely connected questions.

The main question that lies behind the Christological Controversy is: What is the most basic human problem? From what do we need to be saved? Our answer to this question obviously will have an important bearing on what we think Jesus Christ does to save us. To a great extent, our view of our condition will establish how we view our salvation and how Jesus brought it about. Although it may be an oversimplification, most students who study this period agree that there were two major ways to approach the issue: the method prevalent in Alexandria, Egypt, and that method adhered to by some in the rival city of Syrian Antioch in modern southeastern Turkey. For both schools, salvation itself was at stake.[1]

The Alexandrian View

We already have discussed how Athanasius viewed the human predicament. He taught that our separation from God—the source of life—has subjected us to dissolution, decay, and death. The human problem is decay. The solution is a reestablishment of the lost unity with God. In His incarnation, death, and resurrection, Jesus Christ has reestablished that unity and opened the door to salvation for us. Because the divine and human are united in Him, we, too, can have our relation to God restored. Our lives, like His, can be permeated by God, like "iron in the fire," until we can glow, body and soul, with His grace.

This view still has important advocates, especially in the Eastern Orthodox churches. An anecdote may make its implications clear. In *The Brothers Karamozov* by Russian author Fyodor Dostoevsky, the young, pious Alyosha has his first crisis of faith when Father Zossima, his spiritual mentor, dies. The problem arises when Father Zossima's body begins to putrefy and does so sooner than most. Because the good father was saintly, Alyosha took it for granted that his body would be spared from the usual tendency to decay. Because this did not happen, Alyosha's faith—the belief that even the body of a holy man is permeated with God's grace and wholeness—was challenged, and he was thrown into confusion. Anything that threatens to dissolve this union in Christ also threatens our salvation and must be rejected immediately. This attitude was typical of most Alexandrians.

With such a view, clearly Jesus' divinity must so thoroughly permeate His humanity that that humanity is lifted up and transfigured until it is totally in harmony with the God within. The saints also, because of Jesus, grow in the same direction. There is a tendency here to view the humanity of Jesus as so taken up in His divinity that it is no longer really human. As with most ideas, it could be taken to extremes. One person who did just this was Apollinaris, and it was he who started the ball rolling on the divisive debates concerning the person of Christ that would ensue.

Apollinaris

Apollinaris of Laodicea (ca. AD 310–ca. AD 390) was one of the more able and influential theologians of his day. Along with Athanasius, he was a staunch supporter of the use of *homoousion* against all its opponents. Equally as strongly he rejected any kind of total identity of Father and Son as in Sabellianism.

As an Alexandrian, however, Apollinaris also was concerned with proclaiming the unity of man and God in Jesus in the strongest possible terms. One way to accomplish this was to assert that the Word actually takes over the highest parts of Jesus' human nature—his mind or soul, his character—so there is really no human person in Jesus because it is replaced by the Word. What remains of that human person is only the body or flesh and those aspects of human life associated with the flesh. This is usually referred to as the "Word-flesh" Christology, as opposed to the "Word-man" Christology of the incarnation.

Apollinaris was adamant that Jesus was not a complete human being. If He were, there would be two subjects in one person: the Word and the human. For Apollinaris this was an outrageous concept. Christ is intellect with human flesh. The Lord does not empty Himself by changing. He is only clothed with human flesh.[2]

It is understandable that most Alexandrians tended in this direction. After all, Arius was a member of this group. Because he believed the Word was the center of Jesus' consciousness and underwent all the changes in Jesus' life, Arius logically concluded that the Word must be changeable and therefore only a creature. Athanasius also teetered near the edge of this precipice. In his writings he almost always refers to the human body or flesh, seldom to the full humanness of Jesus. Athanasius did, however, eventually break with Apollinaris on this matter.

Apollinaris's basic teaching was initially based on a soul-body view of human nature. He asserted that the Word replaced the soul of Jesus. As time went on, Apollinaris evidently adopted a different view of humanity, one in which we have a body, a soul, and a rational soul. Now Apollinaris sees the Word as replacing only the rational soul. Regardless of what was replaced, the mover, the core personality of Jesus, was not human but the Word.[3]

Understandably, reactions against Apollinaris were swift in coming from pope and councils. The main objections to his teachings were that it was almost a return to Gnostic Docetism, in which the true humanity of Jesus was denied. Second, if Jesus lacked the rational soul that we all have, He actually was a lesser being than we are. Third, Apollinaris's teaching distorted the portrayal of Jesus in the Gospels. Most important, the Church believed that only what is united to God can be saved. The result of such a teaching is that if Jesus does not have a rational soul, then the highest in us—and that which is in most need of salvation—cannot be saved.

Among those who attacked Apollinaris were the Cappado-cians. Gregory of Nazianzus put the matter succinctly: "For that which He has not assumed He has not healed; but that which is united with His Godhead is also saved."[4]

The Nestorian Controversy

Some churchmen at Antioch took a different view of our human predicament, thus they had a different view of who Jesus was and what He accomplished on our behalf. As they saw it, our problem is a deep-seated moral weakness or perversity of the will. Having turned away from God, we have become incapable of being either happy or good. It is therefore imperative that a real human being should come and restore the goodwill that was lost in Adam. Jesus, of course, is that human being. Like Irenaeus, they see Jesus Christ as the Second Adam, the man who faces temptations but with the power of God obeys the Father in all things, both according to God's plan to save the world and according to his daily thoughts, words, and actions.

Of greatest importance for those in Antioch is that the deci-sions made by Jesus be real human decisions. Anything less would be mere play-acting. If the most basic moving force in Jesus is the Word and the Word alone, then no human act of will is involved and our moral illness is not healed. Although God is certainly pres-ent in Jesus, He cannot be present in such a way that Jesus' own human decision-making powers are usurped by the Word or dominated by it. Therefore the unity of God and man in Jesus Christ must not be of a kind that would cancel out His full human nature. Some distance between the two must be maintained. Theodore of Mopsuestia followed this theological line of reason-ing. He was not shy about insisting that the Word indwelt in a real complete man, who grew in maturity and wisdom. The idea of the two natures being mixed together or confused with each other was anathema to Theodore.[5]

As with the Alexandrians, the ideas of some at Antioch had the possibility of being taken in dangerous directions. In particular, it was easy to drift into seeing the two natures of Jesus as being so independent of each other that no central person holds them together. Thus Jesus would be a kind of walking duet or a dialogue between two persons.

So we have two competing understandings of the person and work of Jesus Christ, each seeing the opposing position as threatening to its understanding of salvation. The Christian thinkers at Alexandria, who believed that only the strongest kind of unity with God could cure human corruption, saw in the position of Theodore and others at Antioch a denial of that unity. Meanwhile, some Antiochenes believed that their counterparts at Alexandria were depriving Jesus of that human will that brings about our restoration.

Added to this complex disagreement was a jealousy on the part of some in Alexandria toward Constantinople and its church leaders. The Council of Constantinople in AD 381 had, among other things, declared that Constantinople should have a rank in the Church second only to Rome. The church in Alexandria had a glorious history and was understandably miffed by being replaced by such an upstart patriarchate. Far more serious to the Alexandrians was the tendency of the new archbishop of Constantinople to follow the "separatist," or Antiochene, view of Jesus Christ. When Nestorius, a proponent of this position, was made patriarch of Constantinople, Cyril, the patriarch of Alexandria, cast a wary eye upon the new arrival. Cyril's own view of Christ was "one incarnate nature of the divine Word."

It was the misfortune of Nestorius to assume the episcopal seat of Constantinople at a time when his region was embroiled in a raging controversy. It concerned the proper title to be given to the Virgin Mary. Was it legitimate to call her *Theotokos*? That term, used especially in the Greek Orthodox Church to this day, is often translated as "Mother of God" but may also be rendered as "God

Bearer." Whatever is said in Christian theology about Mary is always a reflection of our views about Jesus Christ; so it was also at that time and place. Nestorius decided, as Theodore had, that such a title was inappropriate because it did not properly distinguish between the divine and the human in Christ, a distinction important to people who followed his theological reasoning. God was not born in time; the Creator was not formed in the womb. For Nestorius, *Christotokos*, or "Christ Bearer," seemed more appropriate.

In defending his objection to *Theotokos*, Nestorius offered clear reasons: We, the children of Adam, owe a debt to God. This is the debt of a righteous life. It can only be paid by one of the same race that fell. It is Jesus Christ who paid it by His human obedience. If He were not fully human, or if He were of another nature than we are, this debt could not have been paid. Therefore, to deny the full humanity of Jesus does away with our salvation.[6]

A second aspect of Nestorius's thought is also important and dovetails with his insistence on the free decision-making powers of the human Jesus. Here we find that he shares some elements of the theologies of both Arius and Athanasius. Like Arius, Nestorius was deeply concerned with preserving the absolute unchangeability of God, which meant that, in his eyes, God could never be directly involved in the changes that are part and parcel of this world. For Arius (and Nestorius), this meant the Word, united with the human Jesus, could never be thought of as divine. Jesus was a creature. Like Athanasius, however, Nestorius insisted that this Word was truly divine. Therefore, to preserve God's impassibility, his inability to suffer, Nestorius separated the Word not from God, but from the human Jesus, who was born, suffered, died, etc.[7] Thus Nestorius is everywhere consistent. The human Jesus must be severely distinguished from God so His free will can be preserved. At the same time, the divine Word, to preserve its unchangeability, must keep its distance from the humanity.

Understandably, the Alexandrians were outraged at what they perceived to be a denial of what was basic to the Christian faith. They applauded the title *Theotokos* because it affirmed the unity that was so crucial to their understanding of salvation. In their minds, the unity of God and man in Jesus Christ was so close that when Mary bore Jesus, she must of necessity also have borne God. Cyril quickly took up his pen and issued twelve anathemas against the threat coming from the north. He condemned those who divide Christ into two *hypostases* and strongly defended the title *Theotokos*, affirming the close unity, which was so important to the Alexandrians.[8]

Theodoret, a friend of Nestorius, was quick to respond to Cyril's writing.[9] He acknowledged that the title *Theotokos* could be used for Mary not because she gave birth to God, but because she was mother of the man who was united to God. For his part, Theodoret vigorously opposed any suggestion that there was a mixture of God and flesh, which would destroy the individuality of each nature. To speak of two *hypostases*, he said, is not only not ridiculous but also is absolutely necessary.

As usual, appeals were made to emperor and pope, and finally a council was held at Ephesus in AD 431. Eventually scholars would name it the Third Ecumenical Council. But this assembly was plagued with controversy and division. The Alexandrian delegation arrived on time for the council, but most of Nestorius's supporters were delayed by bad weather. Cyril and his entourage decided to proceed with the meeting without them. Nestorius had refused to attend, so the council deposed him. When Nestorius's supporters finally arrived, they held their own council, which condemned Cyril. The emperor and the papal delegation sided with Cyril, and he was restored to his position, and Nestorius was declared to be deposed.

Nestorius, Antioch, and Constantinople had been defeated, and Alexandria had been vindicated. But on a deeper level, neither side was satisfied, and a rift between two major centers of the

Christian faith persisted. Attempts at reconciliation were made. John of Antioch sent a letter to Cyril explaining the Antiochene position in way that he hoped would be acceptable to the Alexandrian patriarch. Although he insisted on the completeness of both natures, John was willing to confess that there is one Christ and Lord. In accordance with this union, it is allowed, he said, to use the title *Theotokos*. Cyril was delighted and replied with joy and thanks. The controversy was over, or so it seemed.[10]

The Eutychean Controversy

The debate concerning the person and work of Christ erupted again when, upon the death of Cyril in AD 444, Dioscurus succeeded him. As many scholars have noted, this man had all of Cyril's faults and few of his virtues. He wished for nothing less than total victory over his adversaries and evidently was not too concerned about how he brought about that victory.

Eutyches and the Second Council of Ephesus

Dioscorus's opportunity for victory came during a debate with Eutyches, a monastic leader who, though situated in the area of Constantinople, was a firm advocate of the most extreme version of the Alexandrian position concerning the nature of Christ. Flavian, the archbishop of Constantinople at the time, condemned Eutyches for refusing to assert that Christ's humanity is *homoousios* ("one substance") with ours and for claiming that He was of two natures before the union but of one nature in the incarnation. This view is usually referred to as Monophysite, or belief in the "one nature" of Christ.

Both sides in the debate appealed to Rome. Pope Leo I answered with his own view, which was standard in the West. In the document known as Leo's *Tome*,[11] the pope asserted that Christ has two natures in one person. Leo stated his belief that though born of a virgin and sinless, this did not mean that Christ was of a different nature than ours. It was equally perilous, Leo said, to believe that Christ is simply God and not a human being or a mere human being and not God. Leo roundly condemned Eutyches and his views. Thus Rome, which had previously sided with Alexandria against Nestorius, was now affirming a position closer to that of Antioch.

Dioscorus insisted that the emperor, Theodosius II, call another council. It met in Ephesus in AD 449. It was an entirely one-sided affair. Eutyches was restored and Flavian deposed. There was some violence. Flavian later died. Leo's *Tome* was not even allowed to be read, and the pope was outraged. He refused to accept the findings of the council, calling it a synod, "not of judges but of robbers."[12] This council is not one of those given the status of "ecumenical."

Chalcedon

In the year following the Second Council of Ephesus, Theodosius II fell off his horse and died from his injuries. He was succeeded by Marcian and Pulcheria, whose sympathies leaned much more toward Antioch than had been those of their predecessor. They called a council to meet at Chalcedon, a city near Constantinople, in AD 451. Scholars have identified this gathering as the Fourth Ecumenical Council. Its confession of faith tried to reconcile the two opposing views of the nature of Christ. It wove together material from Cyril, John of Antioch, and Leo's *Tome*:

> Following the holy Fathers we teach with one voice that the Son [of God] and our Lord Jesus Christ is to be confessed as one and the same [Person], that he is perfect in Godhead and perfect in manhood, very God and very man, of a reasonable soul and [human] body consisting, consubstantial with the Father [*homoousian to patri*] as touching his Godhead, and consubstantial with us [*homoousian humin*] as touching his manhood; made in all things like unto us, sin only excepted; begotten of his Father before the worlds according to his Godhead; but

in these last days for us men and for our salvation born
[into the world] of the Virgin Mary, the Mother of God
[*theotokos*] according to his manhood. This one and the
same Jesus Christ, the only-begotten Son [of God] must
be confessed to be in two natures, unconfusedly,
immutably, indivisibly, inseparably [united], and that
without the distinction of natures being taken away by
such union, but rather the peculiar property of each
nature being preserved and being united in one Person
and subsistence, not separated or divided into two persons, but one and the same Son and only-begotten, God
the Word, our Lord Jesus Christ, as the Prophets of old
time have spoken concerning him, and as the Lord Jesus
Christ hath taught us, and as the Creed of the Fathers
hath delivered to us.[13]

Notice how the Council of Chalcedon attempts to find a
balance by weaving together the major concerns and beliefs of
both sides. Its affirmation is not either/or but both/and. Any
either/or question is met with a simple yes. Is Jesus Christ God or
man? The answer is yes. Is He one person or is He two natures?
The answer is yes. Notice also the four adverbs of Chalcedon:
unconfusedly, immutably, indivisibly, inseparably. On the one hand
we are not to conceive of the Lord as being a mixture of the two
natures or that one nature is changed into another, the two ten-
dencies of Alexandria when taken to extremes. On the other hand,
we are not to divide or separate the natures, the comparable tendency of Nestorius.

The Definition of Chalcedon has become the standard way
of understanding Christology in most of the Christian world even
to the present day. Eastern Orthodox, Roman Catholic, and most
Protestant churches subscribe to it, but not without a heavy cost:
the permanent schism of whole sections of the Church. The
Nestorians, who already had been driven from communion with
the rest of the churches in the Roman Empire, moved to Persia
and formed their own church that subsequently existed under

Islam and continues today as a scattered faith community. But the primary and persistent troubles that followed Chalcedon came from the Alexandrians, who felt they had been ambushed at the council and that far too much had been granted to their opponents, who were all heretics in their eyes. It seemed to the Alexandrians that the Definition of Chalcedon affirmed two Christs.

After Chalcedon

The reaction to the council's decision in Alexandria was swift and violent. One patriarch was lynched, and street riots had to be put down by imperial troops. The Monophysites (the name given to the advocates of the unity of Christ's person, though some object that this title is an oversimplification) were enraged. They continued to insist that Jesus had a true human nature, but it was so permeated by the Word that it was divinized.

A series of Roman emperors struggled vainly to placate the Monophysites. In AD 482, Zeno tried to solve the problem by essentially avoiding the whole issue, proclaiming that the creeds promulgated at Nicaea and Constantinople were sufficient for the faith. This satisfied many in the East, but it offended the supporters of Chalcedon, particularly those in Rome.

The emperor Justinian entered the fray in AD 544 by issuing a proclamation condemning three of the leading theologians of Antioch from earlier times, the so-called "Three Chapters," the writings of Theodore of Mopsuestia, Theodoret's writings against Cyril and the letter of Ibas to Maris the Persian. This did not satisfy the Monophysites, but the supporters of Chalcedon were again offended. Justinian then resorted to calling another council to be held in Constantinople in AD 553. Scholars have named it the Fifth Ecumenical Council. This council approved Justinian's condemnation of the Three Chapters, and a reluctant Pope Vigilius was pressured into approving this condemnation.

During this period, the able theologian Leontius of Jerusalem asserted that the humanity of Jesus did not have its own *hypostasis* but existed in the *hypostasis* of the Word. This teaching did not assuage the feelings of the Alexandrians. In fact, nothing did any good. The Coptic churches—those associated with Alexandria—broke off communion with the rest of Christendom and have been "separated brethren" to this day. While their opponents labeled them Monophysites, the Alexandrians responded by calling the imperially sanctioned Christian church, from which come the Roman and Greek churches of today, Melkites, which can be loosely translated "European imperialists."

One or Two Wills?

The Monophysite Controversy may have been "settled"—only by schism, to be sure—but again questions arose that led to more squabbling in the Christian Church. Sergius, a patriarch of Constantinople, suggested a solution to the continuing schism. He felt that all could agree to "one energy." Upon receiving this proposal, Pope Honorius chose rather to speak of "one will." Thus heated debate ensued over whether Christ had one or two wills.

Clearly, those who were interested in emphasizing a strong union of the two natures so Christ's human functions were drastically reduced would advocate one will. Others strenuously objected. Among those who held out for two wills was a succession of popes, including Martin, who was abused, exiled and later died; and the monastic theologian Maximus, who was not only thrown into exile but his tongue was ripped out and his hand cut off. But Maximus held firm, thus earning his title, "the Confessor."[14]

The eventual solution harkened back to the Council of Nicaea. God has one nature and three persons. He has one will. Therefore will is a function of nature, not of person. Because Jesus Christ has two natures, He must have two wills. This was the decision of the Sixth Ecumenical Council held in Constantinople in AD 680–681 (also known the Third Council of Constantinople). According to the assembly, Christ has two wills, with the human will obediently following the divine will. Beyond the metaphysical speculations involved in the question of how many wills Christ possesses were matters of more practical import for the Christian life. Those who stressed the unity to be found in the incarnation tended to neglect the actual human events in the life of Jesus. The council balanced this tendency by reaffirming Christ's humanity, thus bringing the incarnation back "down to earth," if you will.

We began this chapter by commenting that one approach to understanding these Christological debates is to see the parallel questions concerning our own nature and the way of life of the believer. The Sixth Ecumenical Council of Constantinople might suggest the following as our own prescription for the Christian life: not that we sacrifice our human wills but that they obediently follow the will of God.

The Iconoclastic Controversy

One more series of events needs to be treated to complete this complex chapter: the Iconoclastic (picture-breaking) Controversy. From the earliest times of the Church, Christians have had a divided mind about religious imagery. Some, pointing to the prohibition of graven images in Exodus 20:4, see icons, which are stylized paintings or other artistic representations of biblical persons and events, as an encroachment of pagan idol worship into the Christian faith. Others maintain that such pictures can be helpful to believers by pointing them to a deeper spiritual reality. The church of the eighth century displayed this same ambiguity.

The issue was raised when the Byzantine emperors Leo II and Constantine V condemned icons. Some icons were destroyed, and those who venerated them were severely punished. As usual, resistance and even rioting were the reactions. Among the opponents to the imperial actions were Pope Gregory II and the brilliant theologian John of Damascus.

At this time, John lived in an area controlled by Muslims, who forbade any images for followers of Islam. It was within this complex milieu of Muslims and divided Christians that John wrote. John was aware that God had commanded Moses to condemn images. Therefore John insisted that the highest form of worship or adoration was to be given to the invisible God alone. But the invisible had become visible in the incarnation, so humans may draw the likeness of Christ's form. According to John, images, not only of Christ but also of holy persons and places, serve to stimulate our memories and our piety, thus leading us to divine things by divine power. To deny icons is to deny the goodness of God's creation and the incarnation itself.[15]

The battle raged on, but eventually Empress Irene called a council to deal with the matter. The assembly met at Nicaea in AD 787, and scholars refer to it as the Seventh, and last, Ecumenical Council or Nicaea II. The council eventually approved the veneration of icons, while specifying that actual worship was to be given to God alone.

The approval of icons may seem far removed from all of the Christological controversies we have examined, but it is primarily based on the results of the debates, namely, the approved nature of the incarnation. In the eyes of the council, and in keeping with the beliefs of John of Damascus, to deny the possibility of material means, such as art, to be a vehicle of transmitting the spiritual in effect denies the incarnation, denies that the physical body of Jesus can be the bearer of the divine. So ended the Christological controversies with all of their brilliance of logic and argument, their piety, and their violence and skullduggery.

4

The Controversy over Grace: Augustine and Pelagius

The background now shifts from the Eastern, Greek-speaking world to the Latin West. Although the West was involved in the great debates about the person and work of Christ, the driving force of these controversies almost always came from the East. The Pelagian Controversy, however, was an almost entirely Western affair, which makes it unique. It also was centered on the believer, another unique feature. The debates and controversies we have studied to this point all had clear implications for the Christian life, but now the Christian life occupies center stage. The overarching question in the Pelagian Controversy is always: What makes the Christian life possible? The focus of this new debate was about humanity, its problems and solutions. Clearly, this, like so many other questions, inevitably leads back to the person and work of Jesus Christ. After all, Christ and the Christian cannot be separated.

The controversy over grace entangled two dedicated, brilliant men in arguments that have had a profound influence on Western piety, both Catholic and Protestant. The controversy and its resolution has shaped the ways in which Western Christians view ourselves and our faith, as well as how we read the Bible. The two men are Augustine, the bishop of Hippo Regius in North Africa (354–430), and Pelagius, a moral reformer from the British Isles (flourished 390–418), along with his followers.

Augustine

The Eastern church could rightly boast of a whole host of influential thinkers whose ideas gave shape to Christian doctrine. But the West has one whose singular impact influenced all that followed in its tradition: Augustine of Hippo. His massive body of work includes scriptural commentaries, moral treatises, sociological and theological works, numerous letters, and much more. In the Middle Ages a quote from Augustine could settle most arguments on almost any issue. During the Protestant Reformation, both sides cited Augustine to bolster their positions. The Russian and Eastern Orthodox Churches, on the other hand, have not treated him with such deference throughout history.

The period in which Augustine lived was turbulent, to say the least. During his lifetime, Christianity was made the official religion of the Roman Empire, the first Council of Constantinople was held, and the Christological controversies were in full swing. Meanwhile, the Roman Empire was sagging and near collapse. The Visigoths ravaged the East, headed west, and eventually sacked Rome in AD 410. Other "barbarian" tribes began to run amok in the formerly Roman territories of Spain and North Africa. As Augustine lay dying in Hippo Regius, the city was surrounded by the Vandals, who eventually captured it. Classical civilization was dying, and what we have come to call the Middle Ages was beginning. Augustine has been called the last classical man and the first medieval man.

We know more about Augustine's personal life than we do about any other Early Church father. We have this information because in his *Confessions*, he informs us about his growth and development from the perspective of his later theological position.[1] Even as Augustine relates the events of his personal life that he deems important, and even with the dramatic and often tragic occurrences swirling around him, the emphasis is always on Augustine's inner life and its development. This proves important for our understanding of Augustine because there is probably no other thinker whose inner experiences are so closely intertwined with his theology. For almost any issue, Augustine's first reaction is to look into his own soul, then to look to God. We will follow Augustine's pilgrimage so we may better understand his theology.

Augustine was born in Tagaste in the North African province of the Roman Empire. As a young man, he studied in the great city of Carthage. He tells us that he took full advantage of the opportunities to sin that were found in the big city. He felt that he could find happiness only in the arms of a woman. "I loved to love," Augustine said. "I searched about for something to love, in love with loving."[2] Even here we meet the two concerns around which Augustine's whole life and thought orbited: love and happiness. For Augustine, the two cannot be separated. True happiness can be found only in loving the right thing. Loving most the wrong things can lead only to disaster and misery. Eventually Augustine will find that the happiness he sought can be found only in the love of God, but there will be a long road to travel before that discovery is made. Augustine relates how he tried to find happiness in everything that was not God: in sex, in learning, in success, and in friendship. But all these things either disappointed him or were taken from him.

As part of his education, Augustine read a work of Cicero in which the author stated that happiness is found in the pursuit of wisdom. Therefore Augustine followed his pious mother's advice and looked for it first in the Scriptures. But he tells us that he was too proud to accept the humble style of the biblical books, preferring the exalted style of Virgil or Cicero. Augustine turned from the Scriptures to find wisdom in a sect called the Manichaeans, whose beliefs were similar to those of the Gnostics. The Manichaeans were extreme dualists, believing that there are two eternal realities: spiritual and physical, good and evil. According to the Manichaeans, these dual realities are forever at war, and one or the other only temporarily gains the upper hand. As a result of this ongoing war, some of the good reality has been captured by the evil. The Manichaeans believed this mixture of good and evil to be our present world. Therefore God is not responsible for the natural evils we endure; the evil substance is to blame. We, too, are a mixture: Part of us is good (of the same substance as the divine), and part is evil. Therefore we are not responsible for our sins; the evil substance made us sin. Along with their dualism, the Manichaeans were also extreme ascetics, forbidding marriage and the eating of meat. These prohibitions applied especially to their leaders, the elect. Augustine stayed with the Manichaeans for about a decade, only gradually loosing confidence in their teachings.

Eventually Augustine was promoted to a high position as a professor of rhetoric in Milan, Italy. To all appearances, he had everything he could want to make him happy. He was successful in his career as a rhetorician, and he was rising within the ranks of the intellectual class. Augustine had had the best education the Roman Empire could supply, he was surrounded by good friends, and he had a loyal mistress. Yet inside he was miserable. Augustine believed the flesh should be avoided, yet he had a mistress. He had dedicated himself to the search for truth, but he taught his law students how to lie successfully. The Manichaean philosophy in which he hoped to find truth had disappointed him, and he was almost to the point of believing there was no truth.

It was at this point that Augustine came into contact with Ambrose, the bishop of Milan. Ambrose had what can only be called a strong personality, evidently fearing nothing or no one in the defense of the Christian faith. Ambrose had been able to prevail over one emperor who had allowed Arianism to take root in

Milan. He also had forced the great Theodosius I to kneel publicly before him and confess his sins. Ambrose also was a gifted preacher and had considerable knowledge of and appreciation for Neo-Platonism.

Augustine went to hear Ambrose preach, evidently to pick up some pointers on public speaking. However, Ambrose's sermons impressed Augustine, and he began to believe that maybe Christianity was not only for the simple-minded. He started to move in the direction of the Church. Augustine also tells us that at about this time someone placed into his hands some books "of the Platonists," almost certainly works of the philosophers of Neo-Platonism, a school that was in vogue. As he read these works, Augustine's eyes were opened, and his intellectual problems were solved.

The Neo-Platonists saw God as the great One, from whom everything emanated or flowed out in descending order, from highest to lowest. Thus everything ultimately comes from God. For Augustine, this meant there is no evil substance, as the Manichaeans taught. The implications of this belief were enormous for Augustine. If God is the source of everything and God is good, then everything is good. Evil has no existence. Instead, there is only a privation or a lack of good, just as cold is a lack of heat and a shadow is a lack of light. Thus evil choices cannot be choices of evil things, which do not exist. Instead, they are choices of a lesser good. The best choice will be choosing or loving the highest good, namely, God. Finally, happiness is found in the love of God. Augustine became a Neo-Platonist and would remain so throughout his life. When he eventually began writing and thinking as a Christian, Augustine would do so in the terms of this philosophical school. Like Origen and others, Augustine formulated his thinking in terms of his faith, but he also understood and expressed it in the rubrics of what he believed to be the best thinking of his day.

Augustine also notes in his *Confessions* that there was something missing in the works of the Platonists. He says he found in these works that "in the beginning was the Word, and the Word was with God, and the Word was God" and that "all things were made by Him," but he did not find that "the Word was made flesh."[3] Proud philosophers were unable to accept the humble Jesus. Later, Augustine would say that philosophers are the sorriest of men because they are wise enough to see the ultimate goal—the vision of God—but they are too proud to believe in the way to that goal—this humble Jesus.[4]

Augustine had solved his intellectual problems to his own satisfaction, but inside he was still in turmoil. This ended dramatically when a visiting friend told him about individuals who had given up everything for the kingdom of God. Augustine was cut to the quick. How could he, with all his education and advantages, remain spiritually paralyzed while others stormed the gates of heaven? He went into the garden to be alone. He picked up a copy of Paul's letter to the Romans and read: " . . . not in reveling and drunkenness, not in debauchery and licentiousness, not in quarreling and jealousy. Instead, put on the Lord Jesus Christ, and make not provision for nature and nature's desires" (Romans 13:13–14). Augustine said he needed to read no further. He had had a life-altering experience of receiving the grace of God.[5]

Augustine soon resigned his position, and after being baptized by Ambrose the next Easter, he joined a few like-minded friends to form a Christian version of Plato's academy. They devoted themselves to the study of Scripture, dialogue, prayer, and meditation. These were rich years for Augustine, but they were not to last. On a trip to the city of Hippo, Augustine was recruited by the local bishop, entered the priesthood with some reservations and yet, obedient to his vocation, in AD 396 he became sole bishop of the city.

As he looked back on his life in the *Confessions*, Augustine saw it as his own struggle to find happiness in everything that was not God. He had been running from God the whole time until God finally caught him and enabled him to find the happiness he sought. Augustine begins this book with the famous prayer: "Thou hast formed us for Thyself, and our hearts are restless till they find rest in Thee."[6] This prayer was a confession of his own sin and of the grace of God.

During the first few years of his growth in faith, Augustine developed a view of the human condition that would stay with him for the rest of his life. He proposed that there are three levels of reality: God is the highest, the body is the lowest, and the soul is between the two. When the soul is turned upward to God in obedience, it is happy. When it turns itself away from God and toward lower things, the body rebels against it, just as the soul rebelled against God. Thus the soul can become dominated by and enslaved to the very body it was meant to control.[7]

All this is background for understanding the fervor with which Augustine will oppose Pelagius. But there is one more important step to be taken. We can see from the works Augustine wrote during his retreat years and early in his vocation as a priest that he insists that happiness is found only in loving God.[8] During this early period, he also believed firmly that we are fully capable of doing it. We have a free will, so by choosing to, we can love God. It is that simple.[9] Accompanying these beliefs is the idea that, in our pride, we humans want to dominate the world but become "hooked" on it and enslaved to it. Like a young child holding on to the candy, his arm and fist trapped inside a narrow-mouthed jar, we cannot let go. Enthralled with exteriors, we cannot see the God within. In the humble Jesus, however, we can see God outside, which forces us to seek the God within. At this point in his career, Augustine sees Jesus as that exterior teacher.[10]

Because he was a pastor who dealt with the sinfulness of people every day and because of his ever-deepening study of Scripture, especially the Pauline Epistles, eventually Augustine completely reversed his position to state that our will is *not* free.

Instead, it is bound in sin, and we cannot choose the good, that is, we cannot choose God. In one sense our will remains free, but only to chose that in which we delight. According to Augustine, we must already delight in something or we will not choose it. Our nature is corrupted with a kind of terminal spiritual illness, so we delight in the wrong things and do not choose the right things. For Augustine, the human tragedy is that there is only one thing necessary to make us happy and good—loving God. But it is the one thing we cannot do.[11] It is his doctrine of sin inherited from Adam—that is, original sin—that sets Augustine apart from most of the great theologians of the East. They, too, believed that the human race is injured by sin, with its terrible consequences, but they affirmed that the image of God—that is, our rationality and free will—are preserved. The theologians of the Eastern church preserve a somewhat rosier picture of our human race than does the gloomier Augustine.

Where there is a strong doctrine of sin, there must be a strong doctrine of grace to complement it. Thus Augustine's doctrine of grace is as strong as one will find anywhere. According to Augustine, we are in a state of helplessness in our relationship with God. Only by His action are we turned from our pride and selfishness to God. It is God who must turn our hearts, against our own resistance, and give us the love for Him that we lack. One Scripture verse that becomes increasingly important to Augustine is from Romans: "God's love has been poured into our hearts through the Holy Spirit who has been given to us" (Romans 5:5b). The Spirit is given to faith, but even faith is a gift. In other words, it is all grace.[12]

Pelagius

Pelagius[13] appeared in Rome about AD 405, but his reputation preceded him. He was a man of sterling character, and even his enemies found little in Pelagius to criticize. He not only insisted on the highest moral standards for himself but also felt compelled to call others to live the good life as well. Pelagius's whole life and work centered around this call to moral reform, which was certainly needed at the time. The Roman Empire was in a state of moral decay. The blood sports continued, as did the famous orgies. The vaunted Roman virtues of citizenship and honor were now scarce. To make matters worse, the Christian Church had adjusted all too well to these social currents, and it often was difficult to distinguish the average Christian from the average pagan.

Pelagius reminded his fellow Christians that they were to follow Christ as he did. The rich should share their wealth, celibacy was recommended but not required, and social responsibility and self-sacrifice were promoted. Nothing upset this moral reformer more than the belief that such a lifestyle was not possible. The response "I cannot!" was only an excuse for moral laxity, according to Pelagius. He stated that he always accompanied his admonitions with a large helping of hope. Just as a good coach or general would do, he was always ready with a "Yes, you can!" because he knew that every attempt at striving perishes from desperation of attaining.[14] Always ready to accentuate the positive, Pelagius encouraged his listeners to look at their own basic goodness. According to Pelagius, God is good, and He made us to be good. To deny this is to insult God and our own nature, and it pulls the rug from under any striving for improvement. Pelagius pointed to the many Old Testament saints, and even some pagan philosophers, who had achieved moral perfection. Thus he proclaimed that we can do likewise.

Pelagius was well aware that Adam sinned and we sin. But for Pelagius there must never be any suggestion that we have inherited a corrupt nature from Adam. The only thing Adam gives us is a bad example, which has been added to by the accumulated bad examples of others throughout history. Through these bad examples, Pelagius says, we have come to believe that sinfulness is part of our human nature. Instead, what we term "sinfulness" is really nothing more than bad habits. Down deep we are still good, according to Pelagius, and we can draw on our inner resources to do what is right.

In a letter to Demetrias, a woman whom he was encouraging in the monastic life, Pelagius used the analogy of a coin that bears the image of the king to explain the human ability to regain its goodness. The image of the king can be obscured by grime, but with a little polish, the image will shine through again. So it is with us. According to Pelagius, the image of God is implanted in us, but we have obscured it with sin. With a little use of the polish of the Law, however, that image in us will reappear.

Pelagius believed in grace, but in a far different way than Augustine. For Pelagius, it consisted of three things: the gift of our inborn goodness or at least our moral neutrality, the Law that guides us in right living, and the good examples that counter the bad ones, particularly the example of Jesus Christ. According to Pelagius, Jesus was primarily our teacher, not only with His words but also with His entire life. Jesus is a kind of Law incarnate, a teacher and example who exhorts us to follow in His footsteps. Thus Pelagius knows little of the desperate situation of the human heart as it is seen by Augustine. In fact, Pelagius considers such teaching of original sin to be the ruin of moral endeavor.

It is interesting to note how similar Pelagius's views are to those of the early Augustine. Both men believed in free will, and both saw Jesus as an exterior teacher who summons us to make the right choices. But Augustine changed his understanding of sin, grace, and the work of Christ in the life of the Christian, as we have seen. When he read Augustine's *Confessions*, Pelagius came across the prayer "Give what Thou commandest, and command what Thou willest."[15] He rightly took this to imply that we can only do what God commands if He gives us some special gift to enable us to do it. To Pelagius, this smacked of Manichaean moral determinism, and he was upset by it.[16] Thus the stage was set for the battles to come.

The Controversy

These were difficult times for the Roman Empire. The Visigoths had crossed the Danube River and were ravaging the eastern provinces of the empire, even killing one emperor, Valens, in battle, as we mentioned earlier. The Visigoths then moved west into Italy, eventually sacking Rome in AD 410. Other tribes would follow the example of the Visigoths, plunging the European continent into turmoil and sending refugees fleeing southward to Africa. Pelagius and his associate Coelestius joined the refugees and ended up in Hippo. They attempted to pay a courtesy call on Augustine, but he was away at the time.

The first stage of the conflict did not center on Pelagius but on his friend Coelestius, who applied for ordination. Far from welcoming him as a colleague, the Africans brought Coelestius to trial for heresy. The charges against him centered on his Pelagian views. He was accused of believing that Adam would have died even if he had not sinned. This implied that the human corruption that leads to death was an hereditary flaw from creation, not from the first sin. Coelestius also was charged with teaching that Adam's sin injured only himself and that babies are born in the same sinless condition that Adam had before the fall. Further, the Africans charged that Coelestius denied that infants needed Baptism. This charge did not stem from the fact that Coelestius denied that Baptism gave forgiveness but that, being innocent, infants did not need to be forgiven. Finally, the Africans charged Coelestius with believing that the Law is as good as the Gospel for salvation. For his part, Coelestius refused either to affirm or deny any of these charges, thus he was found guilty in AD 412. He subsequently moved to Ephesus, where he was ordained. Pelagius had already traveled east as well, settling in Palestine.

Augustine seems not to have had much involvement in the Coelestius affair, but when he did join the fray, it consumed much of his time, talent, and energy for the rest of his life. The debate also shook the Western church and empire and involved popes, councils, and an emperor.

In AD 414 Augustine sent a letter, carried by his friend Orosius, to Jerome in Jerusalem. This letter expressed Augustine's concerns about the spread of Pelagianism. The next year Jerome and Orosius brought up the case of Pelagius at a diocesan council in Jerusalem, the bishop John of Jerusalem presiding, to hear the charge against Pelagius that he taught that a person can live without sin easily, if he wills. At the council, Pelagius responded that if someone is prepared to strive to avoid sin for the sake of his salvation, God will grant him the possibility of doing so. When it was objected that this left no place for the grace of God, Pelagius condemned all who said that we can advance in virtue without grace. He was clearly sincere in saying this, but remember that Pelagius understood grace to include free will, the Law, and good example. The council took no action against Pelagius and his followers.

Also in AD 415 another council was summoned in Diospolis (Lydda) in Palestine. Again, a number of charges were levied against Pelagius, which eventually were narrowed to three: that he taught that grace was not given for individual actions but consisted of the general endowment of free will; that grace is given for merit; and that if grace alone enables us not to sin, then God would be responsible for sin. Pelagius denied all three charges, and the council acquitted him of all charges.

When news of the Council of Diospolis's action reached Augustine, he was outraged. The best he could say of the decision was that in acquitting the man, it had condemned the doctrine.[17] There was immediate reaction throughout the region of Hippo and beyond. Several councils were held that condemned Pelagianism, and letters were sent to Rome. Pope Innocent I also joined in the condemnation.

But Pelagius and Coelestius were not idle. Pelagius tried to place his views in a more acceptable light. Coelestius traveled to Rome to appeal to the pope. The new pope, Zosimus, was satisfied

with his defense and removed the condemnation issued by Innocent I. At this, outcries again were voiced by the Africans. They
held councils, wrote letters, and engaged in political maneuvers.
Finally, Emperor Honorius stepped in, banishing Pelagius and his
followers. Pope Zosimus then reversed his stand and joined in the
condemnation. As a result, eighteen bishops were banished from
Italy. After this, Pelagius and Coelestius fade from history.

The Central Issues

While all these councils and political maneuverings were occur-
ing, both Augustine and Pelagius were writing, explaining their
views and countering those of the other. Both men were well
aware of the central points in the debate: the goodness or corruption of our present human nature, the freedom or bondage of the
will, and the possibility of moral perfection.

As we have seen, it was crucially important to Pelagius that
our human nature be in a pure state, as it was created. Thus moral
endeavor is possible. It is precisely here that Augustine felt the
attack on Pelagius and his teachings must begin. Augustine was
convinced that his opponent was simply refusing to admit the
empirical evidence that there is something deeply wrong in the
human soul. He considered Pelagius to be too individualistic.
According to Augustine, the whole human race is ill; it is a mass of
perdition. Sin is altogether too pervasive to be a matter of personal
preference.

Augustine is completely convinced that human beings have
inherited their corrupt state from Adam, thus we are much more
than simply imitators of him. Augustine uses various means to
explain how this sorry state is passed on to us; most explanations
involve poor fifth-century biology and poor biblical exegesis. Basi-
cally, Augustine hearkens back to his earlier belief that when the
soul turns to the body in disobedience to God, the body in turn
rebels against the soul. It is through this body (or third state of
reality, for Augustine) that corruption is passed on. That is, it is

passed on through sexual intercourse.[18] However, Augustine rejects the accusation made by Pelagius that he despises creation and the human body. It is not the physical sexual act that is evil, according to Augustine. Rather, it is the corruption of the soul that he calls concupiscence, the lust for domination, that infects all our actions, including the sexual act.[19]

Going on the offensive, Augustine chastises Pelagius for not admitting the illness, thus depriving human beings of the cure. He reminds the Pelagians that the discussion is not about God's creation but about its corruption and cure. Grace is not nature, according to Augustine, it is aid given to a corrupted nature: "Man's nature, indeed, was created at first faultless and without any sin; but that nature of man in which every one is born from Adam, now wants the Physician, because it is not sound."[20] Augustine insists that Pelagius keep to the subject, which is the cure, not the constitution of the human nature. Augustine also reminds Pelagius that one does not deny the created goodness of human nature by admitting the illness. Augustine tells the Pelagians: "Not that by nature grace is denied, but rather by grace nature is repaired."[21] For Augustine, the repair, the healing, can come only by being incorporated into that sinless body of the God-man, Jesus Christ.

The second area of sharp disagreement between these two men was on the issue of free will. This stood at the heart of everything Pelagius believed and taught. According to him, salvation depended upon our keeping of the Law, and keeping it was possible only because we have a free will. This was one area in which Pelagius would allow no compromise, but it flew in the face of everything Augustine had experienced and believed. For Pelagius, the will is the hope of humanity. For Augustine, it is humanity's problem.

In Augustine's mind, the Pelagians made a basic mistake by believing that a free will is one that is neutral, one that can make a choice in either direction for every new opportunity. Augustine believed the soul is free to choose only one way or the other—to choose good or evil. Unfortunately, evil is the direction the soul takes. Also, Pelagius thinks that because the will can ruin us, it also can help us. Obviously, Augustine rejects this belief completely.[22]

As we have seen, there is a sense in which Augustine believes that the will is free. It is free to choose whatever delights it. The delight must come first, and the choice follows. Unfortunately, we now delight in the wrong things, thus we choose the wrong things. According to Augustine, only if God steps in with His Holy Spirit can this illness be healed and our choices corrected:

> A man's free-will, indeed, avails for nothing except to sin, if he knows not the way of truth; and even after his duty and his proper aim shall begin to become known to him, unless he also take delight in and feel a love for it, he neither does his duty, nor sets about it, nor lives rightly. Now, in order that such a course may engage our affections, God's "love is shed abroad in our hearts," not through the free-will which arises from ourselves, but "through the Holy Ghost, which is given to us."[23]

God makes us lovers of Himself. The Holy Spirit is given to faith, but even faith is a gift of God! He personally works our will to believe. We turn to God, but He affects even the turning. Thus even our conversion to faith cannot be used as a merit that deserves God's salvation. It is all grace. Augustine reminds his readers that if grace (*gratia*) is not *gratuitous*, then its meaning is taken away.[24]

Concerning the Law, Augustine avers that sometimes we seem able to keep it, but we do so only resentfully and according to the letter of the Law. When we do seem to achieve this goal, it only increases our pride, the very sin that requires a cure. According to Augustine, unless our concupiscence is healed, the Law only increases our desire to express our unbounded freedom by violating it: "The letter of the law, which teaches us not to commit sin, kills, if the life-giving spirit be absent, forasmuch as it causes sin to be known rather than avoided, and therefore to be increased rather than diminished, because to an evil concupiscense there is now added the transgression of the law."[25]

The third item of disagreement concerns the possibility of perfection. This belief was important for Pelagius because striving for perfection would be difficult or impossible if the goal were not obtainable. Augustine, of course, stridently disagrees. The bishop of Hippo is convinced that there never has been a sinless man except Jesus Christ. If Pelagius can boast of the perfection of the Old Testament saints, Augustine will list their vices. Augustine points out that even Paul cried out, "Wretched man that I am" (Romans 7:24). Pelagius, on the other hand, believes Paul was referring to his pre-Christian days. Even if Augustine will grant the theoretical possibility of perfection, it would only come by grace.[26] For Augustine, our guilt is taken away in Baptism, but the power of sin remains and is only gradually removed. The Christian life is an ongoing struggle against sin.[27]

It may be surprising, but there is one area where the two men agreed. They were both convinced that God does reward us for our merits. For Augustine, these merits themselves are gifts of God, who produces them in us through the Holy Spirit: "Their own crown is recommenced to their merits; but your merits are the gifts of God."[28]

Julian

As Pelagius and Coelestius departed the scene, there arose another of their kind who would take the battle to Augustine: Julian of Eclanum. He was one of the bishops exiled from Italy by Emperor Honorius. Julian was bright, thoroughly dedicated to the Pelagian cause, and aggressive. Many of the debates that he had with Augustine were largely repeats of previous arguments, but Julian went on the offensive and accused Augustine of continuing to be a Manichaean! The charge had the ability to harm the venerable bishop of Hippo. After all, Augustine had been a member of that sect for many years, and it was reasonable that some of its teachings still clung to him. More important, some of Augustine's doctrines could be thought of as being Manichaean: that there is a serious evil present in humans; that sexual relations and marriage are questionable; and, most important, that humans do not have a free will and are constrained to sin by our nature. All these could belong in the Gnostic tradition, of which Manichaeaism was a part.

Augustine rose to the bait and returned the compliment: He charged that Julian and his friends were closest to the Manichaeans. The Manichaeans say that God is not the Creator because He is not responsible for the present world. The Pelagians say that He is the Creator but not the Savior because we do not need divine help to be saved. Both sects dismember the Creator and the Savior. Catholics, on the other hand, say He is both Creator and Savior. Augustine the Catholic, i.e., universal, orthodox Christian, says that he would have perished had not the one who had made him in Adam also remade him in Christ.

According to Augustine, both the Manichaeans and the Pelagians reject grace. The Manichaeans say evil is in us as a part of our nature, thus we cannot be healed. Therefore healing grace is impossible. The Pelagians say that our nature is not evil but is so good that it does not need to be healed, thus grace is unnecessary. Catholics say that evil exists, not as our nature but as a corruption of it. Our natures are capable of being healed, and grace is necessary for that healing. Augustine believes the shoe is now on the other foot, and the errors of the Pelagians have been exposed.[29]

Predestination

Augustine was a radical. His view of sin was radical, so also was his understanding of grace. Many of those who happily followed him were troubled by what they considered to be the extremism of his ideas. It seemed his total reliance on grace left little room for human action and accomplishment. Human beings seem to be as passive as stones. Some of those who followed Augustine's views, yet had serious questions, were monastics whose lives were dedicated to living in a way that would please God. The monastics felt they should correct or admonish one another for their good. If all grace and merit comes from God, why admonish one another to do good? In fact, why attempt to do anything good at all?

These are serious questions, and Augustine felt compelled to respond. He told the monastics that he does not deny the place of admonition in the Christian life or the importance of human responsibility, but he will never agree that grace is given for the merit of the turning of the will. Then grace would not be free; rather it would be payment for a debt.[30] It is God who frees the bound will. Jesus is the most free through His unity with God. He is free not to sin. For us, God operates on and frees our bound will by His Holy Spirit, then He cooperates with the freed will. Eternal life is the gift for a good life, but this gift itself depends on grace. Some persevere in the faith; others do not. Perseverance, too, is God's gift. The beginning, the middle, and the end are all grace, according to Augustine, who says that we do not get grace by our freedom, but we get freedom from grace.[31]

The logic of Augustine's position will drive him into the thorny thicket of predestination, but he does not shrink from this knotty problem. He simply affirms his belief in it. One might say that grace is offered to all, but some accept while others reject it. Not so, according to Augustine! All resist, so it is only by the inbreaking of God's irresistible grace that any are saved. Why God should save some and not others is a question that no one can answer.[32]

The clearest examples of unmerited grace are the baptized infant and the human Jesus. Clearly the infant has never done anything to merit God's acceptance, and the human Jesus certainly did nothing to merit the fact that he should be united to God. Thus even the Savior is an example of grace for Augustine.[33] (It is interesting to compare this teaching of Augustine with Origin's idea that the soul of Jesus did in fact merit this union because of its worthiness in the previous realm.) As to those monastics who wondered if admonition would be worthwhile, Augustine tells them that they are doing God's will by preaching and correcting their brothers. However, their outer words will mean nothing unless God is speaking an inner word in the heart of the hearer. God's action is still absolutely necessary for salvation.[34]

Despite his strong insistence on irresistible grace, there is little or no evidence that Augustine ever taught what has come to be known as "double predestination," in which God selects some to enjoy the blessings of heaven and chooses others to suffer the pangs of hell. For Augustine, we all deserve punishment, but God in His mercy saves some. To put his view somewhat crudely, if we wake up in hell, we have no one to blame but ourselves. If we wake up in heaven, we have no one to thank but God.

The debates concerning Augustine's beliefs and those of Pelagius continued to upset the church. Finally, the Ecumenical Council at Ephesus condemned Pelagius along with Nestorius. Evidently, both seemed, each in his own way, to rely too much on the human side of things. Nestorius made Jesus too independent of God's actions, while Pelagius did the same concerning human beings. John Cassian condemned both men for precisely this reason.[35]

A Western church council in Gaul (modern France) in the city of Orange in AD 527 gave its support, for the most part, to Augustine's teachings. It seemed that Augustine had won the victory. But even those who agreed with his basic doctrines were uneasy about following them to his extremes. Much of the "Augustinianism" of the Middle Ages was Augustine with the rough edges removed. Even some blatant Pelagians thought of themselves as Augustinians. During the Protestant Reformation, both sides claimed Augustine—but only a part of him.

Jesus Christ

As we have suggested, the debates about our condition and salvation lead directly to the issue of who Jesus is and what He did for our salvation. In Pelagius's mind, it was not a complicated matter. Jesus is God's living Law, the teacher and exterior example who can enlighten and inspire us to draw on our God-given abilities and do what is right. Augustine also saw the Savior as such a teacher. But because Augustine was convinced that our problems are much deeper than mere ignorance, he believed that Jesus must do more for us than simply enlighten us. We are desperately ill in the inner person, and we need a physician. Augustine presents us with a rather rich array of ways of conceiving of this healing brought by Jesus Christ.

Of first and greatest importance to Augustine is who Jesus Christ is—the God-man. According to Augustine, in the incarnation, God united Himself with the human nature that has become corrupted so it can be made well. Because Jesus was conceived without lust, without sin, His nature is pure and undefiled. We are quite literally united to this sinless human nature by being incorporated into His body, the Church, through Baptism. Christ is the head; we are His body. The two—our humanity and His—become one flesh, and we are lifted up by His coming down. We are made part of a new humanity. According to Augustine, without this union, and considering our sorry state, we would not be able to imitate Christ's goodness.[36] Because of this humanity, Christ becomes our mediator. Augustine is no Arian or Apollinarian. The Word is God. But what mediates between this God and us is the human nature that has been assumed by the Word. Augustine repeatedly uses the phrase "the one Mediator between God and man, the *man* Jesus Christ."

Who Christ is must similarly be closely tied to what He has done. Our fall was caused by pride—we wanted to play God. In Jesus' humility He heals us by joining with that proud nature.

Thus Augustine could cry out: "God has humbled himself, yet man is still proud."[37] Therefore the humility of God heals the pride of man, which is accomplished not only by giving us an example to imitate but also by instituting a new humanity with a new head.

According to Augustine, Satan is the king of pride, and our own attempts to rise up to be God brought about our fall. Obeying the devil, we have fallen under his control and are in bondage to him. In His humility Jesus Christ lets evil work its worst against Him, even to the cross. David (the humble Jesus) defeats Goliath (the proud Satan).[38] That is, Satan, who holds us captive, makes Jesus pay a price that we deserve to pay, but Jesus, in His innocence, does not deserve to pay. This price is the ransom of His very life that Jesus pays to the devil for our freedom. Thus He literally is our Redeemer (from Latin *re-emereor,* which means "to buy back"). Notice that this is a price paid to Satan, not a price paid to God, which is a thought found in some other early Christian writers.[39]

Incorporated in the new humanity and freed from the clutches of Satan, we are now freed to obey God, that is, to delight in Him and higher things rather than those lower things that we wanted to dominate but which in fact have dominated us. This delight is also from God.[40] Sent from the Father and the Son, the love of God is shed abroad in our hearts by the Holy Spirit who is given to us. The incarnation, the work of the Lord, and the coming of the Holy Spirit are all gifts. Augustine asks, "What do you have that you have not received?"[41]

5

Looking Backward

I f we look back over the history we have just studied, we may
conclude all too easily that the main thing that early Christians
did was fight with one another over the Prince of Peace. Not quite
true. Four debates throughout five centuries is not excessive, especially because they were trying to work out the meaning of what
was dearest to their hearts, the Christian faith. The earliest Christians worked out the doctrines of the faith in ever-new political
situations and amid changing cultural forms and philosophies.
Also, because we concentrated on the debates, we omitted the host
of other things that the early Christians were doing: worshiping,
evangelizing, building, and so on. They also considered many
other aspects of the organization of the Church, such as ecclesiastical authority, how to treat the lapsed, and the proper date of
Easter.

In fact, the early Christians allowed a great deal of diversity
in dealing with questions concerning the human situation, Jesus
Christ, God's grace, and the interrelationship of these. Consider
how utterly different were the approaches of Irenaeus, who
rejected all that he considered idle speculation, and the Alexandrians, who delighted in exactly that type of speculative theology.

Although Irenaeus found every detail of Jesus' life and ministry to be of crucial importance, the Alexandrians had little interest for the details. Or what about the obvious differences between the Eastern Christian thinkers, who insisted that free will and human responsibility remained in fallen humanity, and Augustine, who believed human will to be no longer free? Compare Origen, who believed that Jesus' human soul deserved union with the Word because of previous merits, with Augustine, who insisted that Jesus' union with that Word was the most outstanding example of grace precisely because He had no previous merits.

More important than these disagreements, and more central to the fledgling Christian faith, each early Christian thinker emphasized a different aspect of the life and ministry of Jesus Christ. For one it was a victory won in conflict with the devil, which opens us to the work of the Holy Spirit. For another it is the incarnation that together with Jesus' death on the cross unites us to God and pays the price of corruption that all humans owe. For still another, Jesus' death pays a ransom to the devil. There seems to have been room enough for many views in the Early Church. The controversy ensued only when the respective parties were convinced that something central to the basic Christian Gospel message was being threatened. Then the offending doctrine was challenged and condemned. This means that though the field was large, there was an "out of bounds."

Individuals and whole schools of thought struggled to understand the Christian faith and appropriate its message in their lives. They did so by seeing their relation to Jesus Christ in the way they saw everything else in their life—in terms of their own cultures, with its unique values, norms, and ways of looking at the human situation. These men approached this faith by using the best thought forms, the best philosophy, and the best science of their day. The Gnostics clearly appropriated the syncretism and dualism of their culture. Justin made use of Stoicism, and though Tertullian rejected philosophy, he did so in Stoic terms. Most of the Early Church fathers, including Origen, Athanasius, and Augustine, made use of some variety of Platonism as the most helpful in understanding and explaining their beliefs. Some clearly went too far in this use of a particular philosophical school, as the "down to earth" theology of Irenaeus reminds us.

Despite their differing approaches to the debates of the Early Church, all the "winners"—those whose positions became "orthodox" in the Christian faith and have been handed down to us—were determined to treat with utmost seriousness what was basic to the faith: the grace of God given to us in Jesus Christ. Some stressed the incarnation—the union of God with humanity. Others looked primarily to the revelation given to us in Jesus Christ, who taught us not only by words but also by His example. The cross was important to all of them, but even here there were a number of differing interpretations: The cross was the victory of righteousness or humility over the devil; it was a sacrifice to God or, variously, to Satan. All looked to the resurrection as the bestowal of life. Few limited their theologies to only one of the above emphases; instead, all combined several emphases into a woven tapestry of doctrines. The surprising thing is that with all their differences, these early Christian thinkers tolerated many divergent interpretations within the overall context of the Christian faith.

Combined with these various understandings of the person and work of Jesus, there were parallel beliefs concerning what all this meant for the Christian life, both here on earth and in the hereafter. The idea that the cross was a sacrifice to the Father, so dear to modern Catholics and Protestants, is found in a few Early Church fathers, but not many. Where it exists, the belief is not accompanied by an exclusive emphasis on forgiveness—which everybody, even Pelagius, believed in. More often the emphasis was on grace, which teaches us, uplifts us, frees us, and inspires us. While each of the Early Church fathers saw our human predicament from his own perspective, all of them saw what Jesus Christ accomplished in His life, death, and resurrection as that which changes all aspects of our present lives.

Obviously there also were losers in these debates. Many divergent doctrines fell by the wayside of mainstream Christianity. They were rejected because, in the opinion of those in the mainstream, those who had promoted these doctrines and the doctrines themselves had gone out of bounds. A helpful way to look at this situation may be found in one of Augustine's responses to Julian. Augustine describes what he sees as the errors of two distinct groups: those who make grace of God *unnecessary* and those who make it *impossible*.

Within the unnecessary group we find the Gnostics and the Pelagians. Both believe there is something about human beings that does not need to be saved by grace because that part, that spark, is good enough on its own. The Gnostics believed that in our innermost selves, human beings are already part of the spiritual realm. We have a "spark of the divine" in us. Salvation occurs through a process of self-discovery in which we realize our spiritual nature and our true home. Christ comes to reveal this to us, and in some weak sense, this may be called grace. But He is revealing only what is already true of us. There is no need for a change in our basic nature, which already is spiritual.

The Pelagians, too, make grace unnecessary because they see human beings as so naturally good and uncorrupted that we are fully able to save ourselves without any curative help from God. We only need the Law and good examples. With some effort on our parts, we are fully capable of attaining perfection. We could even place Nestorius in this category because he tended to separate the Word and the human in Jesus Christ to such an extent that he frightened the Alexandrians into believing that for him the human Jesus could function independently of that Word.

A whole host of early followers of Christ went out of bounds by making grace impossible. They did so because they could not abide that God would be active in this corrupt and changing world. Therefore His work could not extend to some aspect of human life, especially the physical body. Therefore they made the creation or the incarnation or both either impossible or irrelevant. For example, the Arians insisted that God is perfect and therefore unchangeable. This led them to promulgate the belief that the Word, which is involved in creation, must not be divine but a creature. The result is that God's grace does not save us; instead, a mere creature does.

Most of those who fit into the impossible category concerning grace take the opposite tack. They do not deny that God is involved in our salvation, but they reject His involvement with the whole of our human nature. Marcion could never be accused of diminishing the impact of grace. However, because he could not hold the Creator and the Savior together, Marcion believed grace could never extend to the created world, including our physical bodies nor even to the body of Jesus. Thus Marcion fell into Docetism. Apollinaris and Eutyches actually affirmed the incarnation but denied either that Jesus was fully human or that His humanity existed in any meaningful way after the union with the divine. Thus grace does not extend to humans as we know them. Many of the Gnostics were able to make grace unnecessary because we are already spiritual; at the same time, they made grace impossible, at least in regard to our physical natures, which they considered unsaveable.

We began this study of church history by backing into it. We started from the present situation and asked how we got here from there. We have seen how traditional Christian teachings have become accepted in the orthodox understanding of the faith. Thus even if we disagree with them in whole or in part, we can at least do so with some understanding of the attempts of the Early Church fathers and their opponents to understand and explain the truth of the Christian faith. But as we read the works and delve into the accomplishments and missteps of the early Christian thinkers, we might also find help from them as we struggle with understanding the Christian faith in our own day. Our problems are not identical, but there are parallels because we face the same ultimate human situation—sin and mortality. By studying the early Christian thinkers, we may save ourselves the trouble of reinventing the wheel. We might be reminded that the Christian faith is an immensely rich thing. Both those who say "only my way is correct" and those who say "anything goes" should take heed lest they lead themselves and others down a path that, knowingly or unawares, ultimately denies the basics of the Christian faith, especially the person and work of Jesus Christ and the importance of God's undeserved grace in the life of the Christian.

We also find in most of the Early Church fathers a serious effort to come to grips with the best that their culture has to offer. They did not shrink from trying to relate their faith in a consistent way with the finest science and philosophy of their day, for example, the Stoic Word; or the Platonism of Origen and Augustine. Those who could not or would not come to some *detante* with their world tended to fall by the wayside for lack of relevance. Yet some went so far in this endeavor that their faith was gobbled up in relevance. The Gnostics are the prime example of this, but questions may still be raised about whether some of the "winners" were guilty of warping the Christian faith by casting it in ways that were not appropriate. We, too, face a culture—especially in the areas of science and technology but also in the areas of ethics and values—that sometimes lends itself to Christian proclamation and practice and sometimes contradicts it. We must be aware that the struggle to interpret the faith within that culture, a struggle of ideas and belief that can sometimes warp the words used to define the faith and create as many problems as it does possibilities, will likely never end, and each generation must do its best in trying to find a faithful proclamation of Scripture. But a look at the Early Church fathers in their attempts at the same thing can remind us that a complete identification with any culture or a total rejection of it are both paths to disaster.

Finally, and most important, we can see that amid all the variety and confusion, despite all the squabbling, accusations, and political intrusions, those who were indeed the shapers of the historic Christian faith that has endured for millennia were the ones who fought mightily to preserve, understand, and apply the oral and scriptural teaching about God and His creation, about the person and nature of Jesus Christ, and about the person and work of the Holy Spirit. The major concern of these Christian thinkers was salvation from the human predicament and the proclamation of the grace of God.

6

Jesus Then and Now

Jesus is still important! Witness the deluge of magazine articles, movies, TV specials, and books being published about Him— some serious, some ill-informed, and some simply off the wall. Most have no discernable basis in fact or reason.

Jesus is still being debated! Learned journals and books continue to argue about who He was, what He did, and the significance of it all. Movie stars, athletes, politicians, and your neighbor are usually not bashful about sharing their particular picture of Jesus. It seems there are about as many kinds of Jesus as one could imagine.

It should not surprise anyone with any level of acquaintance with the Early Church fathers that much of the present talk of Jesus not only disagrees with the opinions of these Christian thinkers but also attacks the core of their positions. Sometimes these contradictions are knowingly developed; sometimes the contradictions are presented without any knowledge of the Early Church fathers or their views. How would these early Christian thinkers react to these criticisms? How would they confront their critics? Of course, we cannot be certain of what they might say in any particular set of circumstances, but from what we know about their strongly held views concerning salvation by grace in Jesus Christ, we can have a good idea of their responses. So we can attempt a mental experiment and imagine what the Early Church fathers might say when facing the modern world and its criticisms. In doing such an exercise, we also might be able to learn from their battles as the same issues emerge in new forms today. Thus we might be able to answer the young lady's question from the preface: "Why in the world should I ever study anything like *that*?"

Of course, anyone is free to join the critics and ignore or attack some or all of the teachings that were formulated by the thinkers of the Early Church. But in doing so, such individuals must admit that they are disregarding or setting themselves against that which a great multitude have held sacred throughout the centuries. In this debate, we can be fairly sure that the Early Church fathers would see most of their modern critics as exactly that which they had encountered but wearing a new dress. There is truly little that is new under the sun.

Criticism 1:

The Early Church Fathers Are too Intellectual in Their Approach to the Christian Faith

Probably the most common and "popular" accusation against the Early Church fathers is that they obscure the Gospel of Jesus by subjecting it to needless and even distorting intellectual formulas and complex creedal decrees. Those who make this accusation are typically, but not necessarily, individuals who are adverse to any and all theological statements of belief. They probably align themselves with a congregation, denomination, or even a non-Christian religion because they feel welcome, the music is good, the morality seems right, there are good programs, or the sermons are uplifting. Perhaps these individuals are even attracted to a group because its people rang their doorbell and invited them to church. For them, belief in some higher power and the dedication to living a good life are enough. Theological niceties are resented and should be avoided. Other, more existentially important matters, are at hand. In fact, much of the contemporary appeal of some forms of Judaism and Islam arises because they have a simple belief in one God, accompanied by an appropriately simple moral code. Thus some churches are tempted to believe that the less theology in which we indulge, the better we can get along with our neighbors in this multicultural world.

Rest assured, however, that the response of the Church fathers to this attitude would be fairly unanimous. On one hand, they would agree that idle speculation into the nature of God and His interaction with the human family can and does lead to disaster. In fact, much of the work of the early Christian thinkers and the decrees of the Early Church councils was accomplished precisely to limit such speculation. On the other hand, the Early Church fathers would just as strongly insist that beliefs *do* matter, that our mind is an important, perhaps central, part of our being and what we believe has a profound influence on our relationships with God and our fellow human beings. Christianity is more than feelings and good works. *What* we think is important too. Further, the people who decry theological statements really do have a theology in their minds, no matter how unreflective it may be. Therefore, we should think through our doctrines and straighten them out from the outset or they can lead us to precisely those entangling speculations we mean to avoid. A refusal to consider a clear statement of one's own beliefs can leave a person open to all kinds of strange and harmful ideas and practices in the future.

For the Early Church fathers, "getting it right" involved the grace of God in Jesus Christ. This was their touchstone. Whatever threatened to deny grace was rejected. This was the major source of those theological formulations that to some seem so burdensome today.

Criticism 2:

The Early Church Fathers Corrupted the Christian Faith by Using Hellenistic Philosophy

This criticism on a more sophisticated level is frequently leveled by members of the academic community, particularly church historians. For more than a century, a host of scholars have insisted that Christian thinkers in the early centuries couched their beliefs in such thoroughgoing Hellenistic terms that the Christian faith itself could not help but be distorted. Hellenistic thought was so inappropriate to the core subject matter of Christianity that its use encrusted the original message to such an extent that the simple teachings of Jesus were in principle obscured. Philosophy trumped Gospel, and the end point is something different from that intended in the beginning.

It is true that most of the Fathers of the Church used Greek philosophical terms and schools to understand and express the Christian faith: Stoicism, Aristotelianism, and especially the various forms of Platonism. It is also true that applying these philosophical forms to the Christian content affected the outcome. But most of the Church fathers were aware of the problem of using Greek philosophy to explain the faith, so they passed judgment on the philosophical systems they employed from the vantage point of that very faith, witness Origen's effect on the growth of Middle Platonism and Augustine's critique that Neo-Platonism neglected the humble Jesus.

However, the main response of the early Christian thinkers would probably be to admit that every thinker uses philosophy and cultural norms to couch his or her beliefs and message. For Christianity, which claims to be universal in application, this is a necessity, whether we like it or not. The question is not whether we make use of these tools but whether they reflect the best and most honest ways of thinking that our culture offers to us. Although not perfect—which the Church fathers knew—the philosophical schools of their day did allow them to present the faith in terms relevant to the world in which they lived.

The Early Church fathers might in fact turn the tables on their modern critics and ask what views of reality influence our modern or postmodern understanding of Christianity. Are we so sure that the present scientific and philosophical worldviews that seem reasonable today will not appear naïve to future generations, who in turn will see us as perverting the faith as thoroughly as we now pass judgment on our predecessors? The problem is endemic to Christianity. Each generation must live in this tension. That the early Christian thinkers saw the world in terms we cannot always honestly accept today does not give us the right to condemn them until we have "solved" the problem in better ways for ourselves.

Criticism 3:

The Early Church Fathers had an Unacceptable Approach to the Bible

From the beginning, the early Christian thinkers understood the Old Testament, the Hebrew Bible, to be God's Word. As the organized church took form, writings were collected and assembled into what became the New Testament. Admittedly, this took place during periods of controversy, especially during the Gnostic and Marcionite struggles. But once the whole Bible was in place, to a man the Church fathers assumed that these Scriptures were sacred and trustworthy. Sometimes they stretched interpretations beyond reasonableness and resorted to fanciful allegory to maintain this position, but maintain it they did. Heretic and Orthodox alike took the Scriptures as the reliable source on which to base theology and stake their lives.

For more than a century now, this reliance on the Bible has been questioned and even ridiculed. Beginning in the latter eighteenth century and continuing to the present, scholars increasingly apply modern scientific methods to the Bible, as they would to any other historical document. Biblical students and groups in almost every denomination raise questions of authenticity and often have decided the Bible must be declared as inaccurate and inauthentic. Most notable in our own time is the "Jesus Seminar." This group has voted on the authenticity of Jesus' sayings in the various Gospel accounts, they search for the "historic" Jesus, and they stir up a great deal of controversy and engender some amount of fear as the promote their findings and their methods. The basis of the Christian faith seems to be at stake.

It is difficult to say how the Early Church fathers would react to this movement within biblical scholarship. On one hand, the Church fathers were serious biblical scholars and might welcome careful and honest attempts to understand the Scriptures. Often they struggled with passages of Scripture they could not fit into their understanding of reality, for example, their often excessive use of allegory to make sense of difficult passages. Again, like modern scholars, the Church fathers made use of many documents that are now considered outside of canonical (universally accepted) Scripture. Both then and now, the question arises concerning which documents have priority, as well as the meaning of Scripture. Thus modern scholarship has little or no advantage over the Christian thinkers of the early centuries of the Church. On the other hand, the Early Church fathers would be genuinely concerned about the apparent tearing apart of what they considered to be sacred. In their minds, one simply could not treat the Bible like any other document.

The response of the Church fathers would certainly center on their central belief in the grace of God in Jesus Christ. The Bible was especially precious to them because it proclaimed the faith. For the Church fathers, Jesus is present on every page of

Scripture. He appears in the revelations of the Old Testament. He speaks in the Psalms. He is Melchizidek, the high priest and the Second Adam. The sacrifices in the temple point to Christ's sacrifice on the cross, and the exodus from Egypt prefigures His ultimate victory over sin and death, which gives us our freedom. The Church fathers might well agree with Luther that Christ is the center of all Scripture. It is faith in this Jesus Christ that the Church fathers were dedicated to protecting.

The question is one of basics. The Church fathers approached the Bible with a belief in God's grace and in the Scriptures as the source of our knowledge of God and His grace. Many modern scholars take a different approach, work from a different set of assumptions, which they use as their lenses to examine the Bible. The Church fathers might well ask whether this newer, empirical method of coming at the Scriptures doesn't leave out important and even crucial aspects of what the writers intended just as much as or more than the earlier allegorical approach.

Criticism 4:

The Early Church Fathers Had too Low an Opinion of Human Nature

Much of the disagreement between traditional theology, as we have seen it in the early Church fathers, and modern theological thinking centers on differing views of human nature and its need for grace. Much of modern ideology—and not only modern ideology—assumes a basic goodness in the human heart, which has little need for grace as the church fathers understood it, let alone any desire for it. Despite our problems, we are healthy enough down deep that we don't need healing, thank you very much! As it has always been, a high view of the human situation brings with it a low estimation of God's grace.

There is another side to this same coin. Positive thinking about the present stage of the human condition likewise perceives little need for a Savior in whom the grace of God acts to forgive, to heal, and to gain victory over bondage to the forces of evil. In fact the proclamation of such need is often resented as an insult to that inner goodness with which we are all blessed. That the early Christian thinkers affirmed such a negative human condition and a need for external help is, for positive thinkers, highly unfortunate. Such modern Pelagianism is endemic to the present theological and cultural scene, especially in the developed West. It is proclaimed by politicians and other societal leaders, at least when it is in reference to *us*, rather than *them*. In fact, for many laypeople and for far too many clergy, belief in the basic goodness of humanity with its accompanying call to a more strenuous moral effort is exactly what it means to be Christian!

It is clear that the early Christian thinkers would completely reject this package. There was certainly a broad spectrum of beliefs among the church fathers concerning human nature and the effects of the fall upon it. Their views ranged from an insistence on the continued existence of free will and reason to the absolute lack of free will and indeed a dedication to doing only what is evil. Yet to a man, the church fathers insisted that the effects of our rebellion against God are dire. The human family has gotten itself in a bind from which it cannot escape by its own best efforts or positive thinking.

The Church fathers might also suggest, with considerable empirical evidence on their side, that our present situation shows no sign of moral progress when compared to their own time. They might point not only to the history books but also to our daily media outlets. Insatiable greed, lust for power, the sexual and economic use and abuse of our fellow human beings, violence, murder, corruption, war—all point to an illness deep in the human heart that any honest evaluation of our existence and actions must sadly affirm. We have an illness that cries out for the forgiveness and healing power of God's grace.

The Church fathers also would insist that our need for grace requires a Savior who will bring with Him that forgiveness, healing, and victory that we so desperately require. We need more than the teacher of Galilee who appeals to our inner moral goodness. We are in desperate need of grace, which is exactly what many of the early debates affirmed. Only God is capable of saving us, so God must be united to Jesus in some unique way. Only that nature that is assumed can be healed and emerge victorious, so this same Jesus must be one of us. The confession of Chalcedon, with its inner tensions and paradoxes, proclaims this message. As Augustine said, those who refuse to look human corruption straight in the eye deny the disease and are depriving us of the medicine to cure it.

There is another view of human nature that has persisted through the ages until today that is similar to that which we have just examined. However, it stems from a different source. This view states that the human soul is not only morally good but also divine. Therefore, our task in life is to make contact with that inner divinity. For example, some who promote the virtues of meditation do so because through this practice we can find that "spark of divinity" that is in each of us. Such views are becoming increasingly popular, especially among those who are ill at ease with traditional historic Christianity.

Almost certainly the Church fathers would consider such ideas to be important challenges to the Christian faith. To them such views would appear as nothing more than warmed over Gnosticism or even Manichaeism. Irenaeus fought against the belief that our souls belong in the divine realm, and he insisted that we are creatures and will always remain so, even when, by God's grace, we are united to Him. Athanasius, who was second to none in declaring the central importance of this union, was equally careful to maintain the line between Creator and creature. The idea that we have some spark of the divine in us and that we only have to realize this is as old as the hills. Such a belief implies that no real change is required in our inner selves; rather, we must realize who we truly are. Yet such an understanding is never affirmed in Scripture, and from the time of the Gnostic controversy to the present day, it has been roundly condemned whenever it has appeared. Human beings are creatures, not God!

One of the consequences of the belief that God dwells within us, in our very nature, is that we don't need the grace that comes with Jesus. Instead, we only need to look within ourselves. Indeed, any attachment to an outer, visible, historical being can only serve as a distraction and an impediment to our all-important inner journey. Docetism is the twin not only of Gnosticism but of many types of mysticism, imported or domestic. It must also be admitted that some forms of Christian mysticism— Catholic, Orthodox, and Protestant—find ways of getting around Jesus.

The early theologians, who often were mystics themselves, insisted with great vigor that the incarnation was central to redemption. Human beings are physical creatures, so is the man Jesus. It is as a man that Jesus teaches, heals, suffers, dies, and rises. In the New Testament and from the time of Irenaeus to the present day, historic, creedal, orthodox Christianity insists that God Himself chose this way to restore His creation.

Criticism 5:

The Doctrine of the Trinity Is a Cumbersome and Harmful Belief

Since its early formulations, the doctrine of the Trinity has remained central to the Christian faith. However, many Christians seem to believe in it because they have been told they should, but they lack any understanding of the importance of this doctrine. They simply believe what they are told, which places them in a vulnerable position when this doctrine is attacked.

We must be very specific: Not only do non-Christian religious such as Islam and Judaism reject the doctrine of the Trinity, but so do Jehovah's Witnesses, Mormons, most Unitarians, and others who claim some connection to the Christian community. They reject the Trinity for several reasons. First, many who deny the Trinity insist on the central importance of Monotheism, the belief that there is one God. To Monotheists, it is the worst kind of idle speculation to proclaim any kind of "threeness" in God. A second attack is not always stated but is perhaps more important in this rejection: that God does not and probably could not act in history in the manner affirmed by belief in the Trinity. At the heart of the attack on the Trinity is a denial of the divinity of Jesus Christ, which is the central and crucial point. In almost every case in which the doctrine of the Trinity is attacked, the need for divine intervention in our human situation is denied, and this denial also brings a rejection of the belief that God Himself accomplished our salvation in this man Jesus. In reaction to such views, the doctrine of the Trinity is central to the Christian faith. As cumbersome as statements of it may be, this doctrine is the ultimate affirmation of God's grace to a needy world, which is why the denial of the Trinity has been viewed as such a threat to Christianity throughout the ages.

The Early Church fathers saw this, and their stumbling steps toward formulating the doctrine of the Trinity were meant to protect what was a most basic doctrine of the Christian faith. As the Cappadocians saw it, God has given us this wonderful creation and our life in it, though we did nothing and could have done nothing to deserve it. In Jesus Christ, God has involved Himself in our human condition for our salvation, again without any merit in us and despite the fact that we do not deserve it. God helps and guides us with His own Holy Spirit and turns us in directions that we could not walk on our own. All this is a free gift, a threefold gift. It is grace. And the wonder of it all is that it comes from the God who is one. The doctrine of the Trinity, as were most of the doctrinal formulations of the Early Church, were the ways in which the Church fathers answered Augustine's question, "What do you have that you have not received?"

A Timeline of Selected Persons and Events in the History of the Christian Church

323 BC

Alexander the Great dies. Alexander conquered all the territory from Greece and Egypt to the borders of India. He spread Hellenism (Greek culture) throughout this territory.

31 BC

Octavian defeats Anthony and Cleopatra at the Battle of Actium. He becomes "Augustus," the first Roman emperor.

4/3 BC

Possible years of the birth of Jesus Christ.

AD 29/30

Possible years of the crucifixion and resurrection of Jesus Christ. Birth of the Christian Church.

AD 50-100

Most or all of the documents collected into the canon of the New Testament are written during this period.

AD 100-200

Height of Gnostic influence on the Christian Church. Gnostics tended to deny the incarnation and that God is the creator.

AD 144

Marcion is condemned. He believed in two gods: the good God who saves us and the creator god who is not good but only just and perhaps evil.

Ca. AD 165

Justin the apologist (a defender of the Christian faith) is martyred. He proclaimed that the Word was present in all wise and pious persons but present in its fullness only in Jesus Christ.

Ca. AD 200

Irenaeus dies. He opposed Marcion and the Gnostics by averring his belief in God's economy, which included the creation, and in the incarnation, centering on the recapitulation of the human situation in Jesus Christ.

Ca. AD 225

Tertullian dies. Unique among the Church fathers because he wrote in Latin, Tertullian was the first to use the word *Trinity*. He also developed the formula of "one substance, three persons" to describe the Trinity, as well as the formula "two natures, one person" to describe Jesus Christ.

AD 254

Origen is martyred. An immensely important theologian in Alexandria, Egypt, he stressed an allegorical approach to interpreting Scripture. His speculative views would intensify later theological controversies.

AD 312

Battle of Mulvian Bridge. Constantine defeats Maxentius and eventually becomes sole Roman emperor. He begins the favorable treatment of Christians within the Roman Empire, and he founded Constantinople as a Christian city.

AD 325

Council of Nicaea. The first of seven ecumenical councils, the Council of Nicaea was called by Constantine. It condemned Arius, who denied the divinity of Christ, and it affirmed that Jesus Christ is *homoousion* ("of one substance") with the Father.

AD 373

Athanasius dies. As archbishop of Alexandria, he was a stout defender of the outcome of the Council of Nicaea and of the use of *homoousion* to describe Jesus Christ. Athanasius was exiled five times.

AD 381

Council of Constantinople. This is the Second Ecumenical Council. It produced the Nicene Creed, known more precisely as the "Niceno-Constantinopolitan" Creed. This creed states belief in the Trinity, including the *homoousion* of Jesus Christ and the Father.

AD 395

Theodosius I dies. He was the last man to rule a unified Roman Empire. A devout Christian, Theodosius outlawed pagan sacrifices, thus establishing Christianity as the official religion of the Roman Empire. He also called the Council of Constantinople.

AD 430

Augustine of Hippo dies. An important theologian of the Western church, he was known as the "Doctor of Grace" because of his strong affirmation of human sinfulness and the need for God's grace. He opposed Pelagius, who stressed human goodness and free will. Augustine's views drove him to teach predestination.

AD 431

Council of Ephesus. Recognized as the Third Ecumenical Council, it condemned Nestorius of Antioch, who had become archbishop of Constantinople. He had been charged with denying the unity of Christ. The council also condemned Pelagius.

AD 449

Another council at Ephesus, though not recognized as ecumenical. It affirmed that there was only one nature of Christ in the incarnation, which enraged the Roman church (the Western church) and others. It has been called "the Robber Synod."

AD 451

Council of Chalcedon. It is recognized as the Fourth Ecumenical Council. Its statement of faith recognizes both the two natures of Christ and His personal unity.

AD 553

Second Council of Constantinople. Also called the Fifth Ecumenical Council, this assembly failed in its attempt to reconcile the Monophysites with the affirmations of Chalcedon.

AD 680

Third Council of Constantinople. The Sixth Ecumenical Council proclaimed that Jesus Christ, who has two natures, must have two wills, with the human will obediently following the divine.

AD 749

John of Damascus dies. This important theologian of the Eastern church was involved in the Iconoclastic (picture-breaking) Controversy. He insisted that when one denies that physical matter can convey spiritual reality, then one also denies the incarnation.

AD 787

Second Council of Nicea. The Seventh, and final, ecumenical council affirmed that though God alone should receive true worship, icons can be venerated.

Brief Glossary of Terms

Alexandrian Christology: The view of Christ's person that stressed the complete union of the two natures, and was suspicious of anything that would tend to "divide" Christ.

Antiochene Christology: The view of Christ's person that stressed the need for a true and whole humanity in Him, and was suspicious of any view that would negate that humanity.

Apollinarianism: The view, advocated by Apollinaris and others, which taught that the Word replaced the highest aspects of Jesus' humanity. This view was condemned.

Arianism: The beliefs of Arius and his followers. They contended that because God is unchangeable, and the Word was involved in both the creation and the incarnation, it must be subject to change, and therefore cannot be God. This view was condemned by the councils of Nicaea and I Constantinople.

Canon of Scripture: The collection of books considered to be authoritative Holy Scripture. Marcion's collection tried to expunge anything Jewish from Scripture, and ended with only eleven books, which were also edited by him. The Gnostics accepted most books that we have today, but gave them their own twist. They also had many additional books in their collection. By about AD 200 the books selected by most of the churches were very much the same as we have today.

Christology: Teachings about Christ. These are found in the New Testament, and were the subject of most of the debates in the Early Church. These debates largely concerned the divinity and humanity of Jesus Christ and the relation of the two.

Diothelitism: The belief that Jesus Christ has two wills to correspond to his two natures. This was affirmed by the Sixth Ecumenical Council.

Docetism: A name given to a number of beliefs that all, in some way, affirm that Christ only "appeared" to be human. This was the view of Marcion and of many Gnostic schools.

Gnosticism: A collective term for a considerable number of schools of thought that were highly influential, particularly in the Second Century. In general, they believed that this evil physical world could not be the work of the High, or good god. Nor could Christ, our Savior, have a real, physical body. Therefore they denied both the creation and the incarnation. Christ saves us by giving us knowledge (*gnosis*) of our true nature and destiny.

Hellenism: In the period of the Early Church, Greek (or Hellenic) culture tended to mix with, and often dominate various cultures in the Roman Empire and beyond. Many schools of philosophy grew up as part of this process and were used by some of the early Christian thinkers. Two of the more important of these philosophies were Stoicism and Neo-platonism.

Homoiousion: The Council of Nicea in AD 325 had proclaimed that Christ is *homoousion* (of one being or substance) with the Father. Some bishops feared that this smacked of Sabellianism, so they preferred *homoiousion* (of like substance). Note that the one letter, "iota," made all the difference.

Homoousion: The term in the creed of Nicaea, "of one being or substance" with the Father. This eventually became the test case for those who supported Nicaea. In the Chalcedonian Confession this same term was used to express Christ's oneness with us.

Hypostasis: The Greek equivalent of the Latin "substantia." Both mean "that which stands under or behind." In the debates following First Nicaea it was sometimes used to refer to the one substance or being of the Word with the Father. Others thought of it as what stands behind our outer appearance, that is, our individual person. This led to a great deal of confusion. The Cappadocian Fathers helped to clear up the confusion by using "ousia" to refer to the divine nature, and "hypostasis" to refer to the individual persons of the Trinity.

Iconoclasm: Literally "picture breaking." The debate over whether venerating icons was idol worship or an affirmation that the physical can be a vehicle of the spiritual, as in the incarnation. The issue was decided in favor of the later view by the second Council of Nicaea in AD 727.

Incarnation: Literally, "in the flesh." It is used to express the belief that in Jesus Christ, God's very Word became flesh.

Monophysitism: The belief that as a result of the incarnation the humanity of Jesus was so infused by His divinity that He had only one, divine nature ("mono," one, and "physis," nature). The belief in this teaching was largely responsible for the Coptic church splitting from the rest of the Christian churches.

Neo-Platonism: One of the many schools of philosophy prevalent in the Roman Empire. It had a strong belief in the oneness of God and that all comes from Him. Therefore, all is good and evil is only a lack or privation. Augustine was highly influenced by them, but complained that they had no belief in the Incarnation.

Original Sin: The sin of origin. That the corruption infecting Adam and Eve at the Fall has come down to all of us, their descendents. Therefore we are turned against God and cannot return to Him without the direct action of God on our hearts, so that we can come to trust Him and Love Him. Augustine was a strong advocate of this position.

Pelagianism: Pelagius believed we are born naturally good or at least morally neutral, so he denied original sin. He taught that we are capable of achieving moral perfection. For him, grace meant our original endowment with reason and conscience, plus the law and the good example of others, especially Jesus, whom he considered to be primarily a teacher and example. These views were strongly opposed by Augustine, and eventually condemned.

Predestination: This belief is a corollary of the belief in original sin. Because we are so thoroughly infected with sin, we cannot take the initiative in returning to Him, but must rely totally on his gracious initiative in our salvation. Therefore He must choose us before we are ever capable of choosing Him. He must predestine us before we ever choose Him. Augustine was a strong advocate of this position.

Recapitulation: The teaching of Irenaeus that Jesus is the Second Adam, who comes to experience all that Adam did, but does it right. He recaps the human struggle against evil but wins, and so reverses the hold that Satan has on the human race.

Sabellianism: (sometimes also called Modalism and Patripassianism) Some early thinkers, such as Sabellius, stressed the unity of God to such an extent that they saw Father, Son, and Holy Spirit as merely three "modes" of the one Divine reality. Their critics labeled them "Patripassions" (Father sufferers) because they believed that the Father suffered on the cross.

Stoicism: One of the many schools of philosophy prevalent in the Roman Empire. They were Pantheists who believed that God is the universe. The beautiful rational organization of the world is

God's mind. They called this rational mind "Word," because, like our words, it is the outer expression of inner thought. Many Christian thinkers made use of these ideas and applied them to Christ. Justin Martyr is an example of this.

Trinity: The term *trinitas* was first used by Tertullian. It became the standard expression for the belief that there is one God in three persons, Father, Son, and Holy Spirit.

Word: In Jewish thought there was a tradition of referring to God's Word. In Greek philosophy, especially among the Stoics it was the mind of God. The Jewish thinker Philo seemed to unite the two. In the New testament, the first chapter of the Gospel of John states that the Word was God and that the Word became flesh. "Word Christology" became a common, but controversial way of expressing the Christian belief in the incarnation.

Notes

Introduction

1. Larry W. Hurdato, *Lord Jesus Christ: Devotion to Jesus in Earliest Christianity* (Grand Rapids: Eerdmans, 2003).

2. *ANF* 1:191.

3. *ANF* 3:17f., 93f., 181f., 269f.

Chapter 1

1. J. T. Nielsen, *Adam and Christ in the Theology of Irenaeus of Lyons* (Assen: Van Gorcum, 1968), 2.

2. John Lawson, *The Biblical Theology of Saint Irenaeus* (London: Epworth Press, 1948, used by permission of the Methodist Publishing House), 119–20.

3. Jaroslav Pelikan, *The Christian Tradition: A History of the Development of Doctrine*, vol. 1, *The Emergence of the Catholic Tradition (100–600)* (© 1971 by The University of Chicago, all rights reserved), 82.

4. Michael Allen Williams, *Rethinking "Gnosticism": An Argument for Dismantling a Dubious Category* (Princeton: Princeton University Press, 1996).

5. Much recent effort is being exerted in the study of Gnosticism. New works are being published with regularity. Two texts that will offer an excellent introduction to Gnosticism and the ongoing study of its tenets are Kurt Rudolph, *Gnosis: The Nature and History of Gnosticism*, trans. Robert Wilson (San Francisco: Harper Collins, 1987), and Bentley Layton, *The Gnostic Scriptures* (Garden City: Doubleday, 1987).

6. *Against Heresies*, I.30.13 (*ANF* 1:357).

7. Robert Grant, trans., *Irenaeus of Lyons* (New York: Routledge, 1997), 22–23. A similar description of the ideas of Basilides, another Gnostic leader, is given to us by Irenaeus in *Against Heresies*, I.24.3 (*ANF* 1:349).

8. Grant, *Irenaeus of Lyons*, 22–23.

9. Beside the mentions of Marcion in the writings of Irenaeus, much of our knowledge of him comes from Tertullian's work, *Against Marcion* (*ANF* 3:269f.).

10. For Irenaeus's views on Marcion, see *Against Heresies*, I.27.1, 3; III.12.12 (ANF 1:352, 434–435). An interesting insight into Marcion's position is found in Andrew McGowen, "Marcion's Love of Creation," *Journal of Early Christian Studies* (Fall 2001): 295–311.

11. *Against Heresies*, IV.33.8 (*ANF* 1:508).

12. We recall Romans 5:12–21; Philippians 2:5–11; Colossians 1:13–20; and Ephesians 5:22–33.

13. *Against Heresies*, III.3.1–2 (*ANF* 1:415). For the content of such doctrine, see *Against Heresies* I.10.1–2; III.12.2 (*ANF* 1:330–31, 429–30).

14. *Against Heresies* III.9.1 (*ANF* 1:422). See also *Against Heresies*, I.10.1–2; III.3.1–2; and III.12.2 cited in footnote 13.

15. *Against Heresies*, II.26.1; II.28.2, 7 (*ANF* 1:397, 399, 401).

16. *Against Heresies*, IV.11.2; V.25.2 (*ANF* 1:474, 553).

17. *Against Heresies*, I.16.3; II.25.3; IV.6.6; IV.11.2 (*ANF* 1:341–42, 396–97, 469, 474).

18. *Against Heresies*, II.13.8–9 (*ANF* 1:375).

19. *Against Heresies*, II.13.8; II.28.4–5 (*ANF* 1:375, 400). See also *Against Heresies*, II.16.3; II.3.2 (*ANF* 1:380, 362).

20. *Against Heresies*, III.25.3 (*ANF* 1:459).

21. *Against Heresies*, IV.14.1 (*ANF* 1:467, 376, 388). See also John 15:16, 19.

22. Dem. 12, as cited in Irenaeus, *The Demonstration of the Apostolic Preaching*, trans. J. Armitage Robinson (London: Society for Promoting Christian Knowledge, 1920) 81–82. All references to SPCK are to this edition. See also *Against Heresies*, V.29.1 (*ANF* 1:558).

23. *Against Heresies* IV.11.2; IV.38.1–3; II.25.2 (*ANF* 1:474, 521–22, 396).

24. *Against Heresies* IV.11.2; IV.38.1, 2–3; II.25.2. See M. C. Steen-

berg, "Children in Paradise: Adam and Eve as 'Infants' in Irenaeus of Lyons," in *Journal of Early Christian Studies* 12, no. 1 (Spring 2004): 1–22.

25. See 1 Corinthians 15:50. Compare Matthew 16:17, Ephesians 6:12, and Hebrews 2:14.

26. *Against Heresies*, II.29.1–2; V.14.4; V.36.1 (*ANF* 1:402–403, 540, 565).

27. *Against Heresies*, III.19.1 (*ANF* 1:448–49).

28. Johannes Quasten, *Patrology*, vol. 1, *The Beginnings of Patristic Literature* (Westminster, Md.: Newman Press, 1950), 311. See also Gustav Wingren, *Man and the Incarnation: A Study in the Biblical Theology of Irenaeus*, trans. by Ross MacKenzie (Philadelphia: Muhlenberg, 1959 [1947]), 201–13. See Dem. 11, where Irenaeus refers to humans as "Godlike" (*theoeides*) and "like" God (*homoios*) (SPCK 80–81).

29. Dem.18 (SPCK 85–86); *Against Heresies* V.16.2.

30. An important contribution to this issue is Jacques Fantino, *l'homme image de Dieu chez saint Irenee de Lyon* (thesis: Saul choir; Editions du Cerf, 1986).

31. *Against Heresies*, V.6.1; V.12.1–3; V.16.2 (*ANF* 1:531–32, 537–38, 544).

32. Dem. 11 (SPCK 80–81); *Against Heresies*, IV.37.1 (*ANF* 1:518–19).

33. Dem. 12, 15, 16 (SPCK 81–82, 83–84); *Against Heresies*, III.23.1; IV.40.3 (*ANF* 1:455–56, 524).

34. *Against Heresies*, III.20.1; V.9.1; V.12.2 (*ANF* 1:449–50, 534–35, 537–38).

35. See *Against Heresies*, III.20.1; V.9.1; V.12.2 (*ANF* 1:449–50, 534–35, 537–38).

36. *Against Heresies*, I.20.3; III.8.2; V.8.2–3; V.21.3; V.24.2 (*ANF* 1:345, 421, 534, 550, 552); Dem. 17–18 (SPCK 84–86).

37. See Lawson, *Biblical Theology*, 147–54; Leonard Bissonette, *Irenaeus' View of Salvation History* (Ph.D. thesis, University of Ottawa/St. Paul University, 1980; Ottawa National Library Microfiche), 182–83. See also Quasten, *Patrology*, 1:295–97.

38. See Louis Brighton, *Revelation* (St. Louis: Concordia, 1999) 2f., 646f.

39. *Against Heresies*, III.18.1 (*ANF* 1:446); see also III.23.1 (*ANF* 1:455–56).

40. Dem. 28 (SPCK 96).

41. *Against Heresies*, V.21.3 (*ANF* 1:550); see also *Against Heresies*, III.8.2; IV.24.1; V.21.1 (*ANF* 1:421, 495, 548–49); Dem. 37 (SPCK 103).

42. *Against Heresies*, IV.38.4 (*ANF* 1:522). See also *Against Heresies*, III.19.1; III.22.4 (ANF 1:448–49, 455); Dem. 31 (SPCK 97–98); Bissonette, *Irenaeus' View of Salvation History*, 188.

43. Dem. 31, 37 (SPCK 97–98, 103); *Against Heresies*, III.18.1–2; III.19.1; III.22.4; IV.33.4; V.12.2; V.14.4; V.21.1; V.24.4 (*ANF* 1:446, 448–49, 455, 507, 537–38, 542, 548–49, 553).

44. Dem. 31, 37 (SPCK 97–98, 103); *Against Heresies*, III.17.4; III.22.4; III.23.1; IV.33.2; V.1.2; V.4.2 (*ANF* 1:445, 455, 455–56, 507, 527, 530).

45. See *Against Heresies*, III.18.7 (*ANF* 1:448).

46. *Against Heresies*, IV.38.2; V.19.1 (*ANF* 1:521, 547); Dem. 33 (SPCK 99–100); *Against Heresies*, V.21.2; V.16.3; V.23.2; II.24.4–5 (*ANF* 1:549–50, 544, 551–52, 394–96).

47. *Against Heresies*, I.10.1; II.11.1; III.12.8 (*ANF* 1:330–31, 370, 433); Dem. 6 (SPCK 74–75); *Against Heresies*, I.22.1 (*ANF* 1:347); Dem. 28, 37, 45 (SPCK 96–97, 103, 110–11); *Against Heresies*, III.18.6; IV.27.2 (*ANF* 1:447–48, 499).

48. Lawson, *Biblical Theology*, 66–67, 188–89.

49. Dem, 86 (SPCK 141). See also *Against Heresies*, IV.15.1–2; IV.24.2; Dem. 24, 28 (SPCK 91–92, 96); *Against Heresies*, IV.25.1.

50. Dem. 35 (SPCK 102). See Dem. 24 (SPCK 91–92); *Against Heresies*, IV.13.1; IV.18.3 (*ANF* 1:477, 485).

51. Wingren, *Man and the Incarnation*, ix, 128; Lawson, *Biblical Theology*, 214–15.

52. *Against Heresies*, III.6.2 (*ANF* 1:419).

53. *Against Heresies*, III.9.1 (*ANF* 1:422).

54. *Against Heresies*, IV.20.7 (*ANF* 1:489–90). See also *Against Heresies*, III.16.9; IV.Preface.4 (*ANF* 1:443–44, 462–63).

55. *Against Heresies*, V.3.1 (*ANF* 1:529).

56. *Against Heresies*, V.33.4 (*ANF* 1:563); Dem. 31–32 (SPCK 97–99); *Against Heresies*, III.16.6; V.16.2 (*ANF* 1:442–43, 544).

57. See, for example, *Against Heresies*, II.20.3; III.10.2; III.20.2; IV.8.2; IV.13.2; IV.38.3; IV.38.4; V.16.2; V.21.3 (*ANF* 1:388, 425, 450, 471, 477, 521–22, 544, 550); Dem. 1f. (see SPCK 69f.); Dem. 3, 31, 56 (SPCK 71–73, 97–98, 119–20). See also Gustaf Aulen, *Christus Victor* (New York: Macmillan, 1951) 34; Wingren, *Man and the Incarnation*, 95; Lawson, *Biblical Theology*, 159–61.

NOTES

58. *Against Heresies*, V.1.1 (*ANF* 1:527–28). See Pelikan, *Christian Tradition*, 144–45, Wingren, *Man and the Incarnation*, 173. See also Lawson, *Biblical Theology*, 235–40, 279–91.

59. *Against Heresies*, III.20.2 (*ANF* 1:450). See *Against Heresies*, IV.38.3–4; V.1.1 (*ANF* 1:521–22, 527–28).

60. *Against Heresies*, V.9.4 (*ANF* 1:535).

61. *Against Heresies*, V.8.2 (*ANF* 1:534). Bissonette, *Irenaus' View of Salvation History*, 190, 195, 211, 286.

62. Dem. 1 (SPCK 70). See references to Beuzart, Werner, and Ritchel in Lawson, *Biblical Theology*, 15–16, 232–35, and his own response, 235–40. See also Wingren, *Man and the Incarnation*, 143.

63. *Against Heresies*, III.5.3; V.1.1; V.27.2 (*ANF* 1:418, 526–27); Dem. 1–3a, 56 (SPCK 69–72, 119–20).

64. *Against Heresies*, I.23.2 (*ANF* 1:348).

65. *Against Heresies*, I.23.4 (*ANF* 1:348).

66. *Against Heresies*, V.29.2; V.31.2; V.32.1; V.33.4; V.36.3 (*ANF* 1:558, 560–61, 563, 567).

67. Aulen, *Christus Victor*, 34.

68. *Against Heresies*, V.21.3 (ANF 1:550). Lawson, *Biblical Theology*, cites the following references to grace in Irenaeus according to categories: that God called us to knowledge of Himself (*Against Heresies*, II.25.3; IV.37.1; II.9.1); that man should know God is a mark of God's great favor toward man (*Against Heresies*, III.6.4); God's grace is seen in His long-suffering in regard to apostasy (*Against Heresies*, I.10.3; III.23.1); through His infinite kindness God calls the unworthy (*Against Heresies*, IV.36.1; Dem. 41); and captive man is rescued according to the tender mercy of the Father (*Against Heresies*, V.21.3; III.20.1; III.23.6; III.25.3; Dem. 60). See also *Against Heresies*, II.32.4; III.6.1; III.18.1; III.19.1; III.20.2; IV.14.1; V.1.1. See *ANF* 1 and SPCK for the multiple references. See also Wingren, *Man and the Incarnation*, 70, 95, 107–9, 122–24, 132–43, 159–70; Aulen, *Christus Victor*, 21–22; Lawson, *Biblical Theology*, 16, 58, 127, 240–51; Nielsen, *Adam and Christ in the Theology of Irenaeus*, 64, 76; and Bissonette, *Irenaeus' View of Salvation History*, 158, 176–77, 261.

69. Much of the material concerning the formulation of the creeds in this entire book relies on J. N. D. Kelly, *Early Christian Creeds*, 3rd ed. (London: Longman, 1972 [1950]).

Chapter 2

1. Origen's entire "system," as summarized above, is found in his *First Principles* in *ANF* volume 4.

2. *First Principles*, II.VI.6 (*ANF* 4:283).

3. Origen, *Epistle to the Hebrews*.

4. Origen, *Against Celsus*, 8.12 (*ANF* 4:643–44).

5. See Pier Franco Beatrice, "The Word '*homoousios*' from Hellenism to Christianity," *Church History* (June 2002): 243–72. Note that Greek does not have a double-o diphthong, so one pronounces the word *homo-ousion* after the similar pattern of English *homogeneous*.

6. Lactantius and Eusebius give us somewhat differing accounts of this vision.

7. Alexander's circular letter deposing Arius can be found in (*NPNF²* 4:69–72).

8. J. N. D. Kelly, *Early Christian Doctrines*, 2nd ed. (New York: Harper & Row, 1960), 226–31.

9. See H. A. Drake, *Constantine and the Bishops: The Politics of Intolerance* (Baltimore: Johns Hopkins Press, 2000).

10. Much of this discussion and the appropriate sources may be found in *NPNF²* volume 14 and in J. N. D. Kelly, *Early Christian Creeds*, 3rd ed. (London: Longman, 1972 [1950]). See also Bengt Hägglund, *History of Theology* (St. Louis: Concordia, 1968).

11. Beatrice, "The Word '*homoousios*,'" has some interesting opinions on what the word might have meant to Constantine.

12. Kelly, *Early Christian Creeds*, 215–16.

13. Kelly, *Early Christian Doctrines*, 247–51.

14. *NPNF²* 4:31–67, 303–447.

15. Athanasius, *Commentary on Luke 10:22* (*NPNF²* 4:87).

16. Athanasius, *Incarnation of the Word*, 4 (*NPNF²* 4:38).

17. Athanasius, *Incarnation of the Word*, 54 (*theopoiethomen*) (*NPNF²* 4:65).

18. Athanasius, *Incarnation of the Word*, 7 (*NPNF²* 4:340).

19. Athanasius, *Commentary on Luke 10:22* (*NPNF²* 4:88).

20. Athanasius, *Commentary on Luke 10:22* (*NPNF²* 4:88).

21. Athanasius, *Commentary on Luke 10:22* (*NPNF²* 4:87–88).

22. Athanasius, *Four Discourses*, I.40 (*NPNF²* 4:370).

23. Athanasius, *Four Discourses*, II.40–41 (*NPNF²* 4:370).

24. Athanasius, *Four Discourses*, II.38–39 (*NPNF²* 4:368–69).

25. Athanasius, *Four Discourses*, I.15.

26. Athanasius, *Four Discourses*, II.18 (*NPNF²* 4:357).

27. Athanasius, *Four Discourses*, II.8; III.34 (*NPNF²* 4:352, 412); *Incarnation of the Word*, 54 (*NPNF²* 4:65–66).

28. Athanasius, *Four Discourses*, II.59 (*NPNF²* 4:380–81).

29. Athanasius, *Four Discourses*, III.24 (*NPNF²* 4:406–07).

30. Athanasius, *Four Discourses*, III.19 (*NPNF²* 4:404).

31. Athanasius, *Four Discourses*, I.8, 30 (*NPNF²* 4:310, 324). See David Brakke, "Jewish Flesh and Christian Spirit in Athanasius of Alexandria," *Journal of Early Christian Studies* (Winter 2001): 453–81.

32. Athanasius, *Four Discourses*, II.20 (*NPNF²* 4:359).

33. Athanasius, *Four Discourses*, I.17, 26 (*NPNF²* 4:316, 321–22).

34. Athanasius, *Four Discourses*, II.38; III.2, 9, 64 (*NPNF²* 4:368–69, 394, 398, 428–29).

35. Athanasius, *Four Discourses*, I.36, 41; II.47; III.32, 51, *et passim* (*NPNF²* 4:327, 330, 374, 411, 421).

36. Tertullian, *Against Praxeas*, II (*ANF* 3:598).

37. LW 40:79–223.

38. LW 40:83.

39. Surveys of these developments can be found in any church history or history of doctrine. Examples include Justo Gonzalez, *The Story of Christianity* (New York: Harper & Row, 1984), 1:173f. and Williston Walker, et al., *A History of the Christian Church* (New York: Charles Scribner's Sons, 1985), 137f.

40. Basil, *Ep.* 236.6 (*NPNF²* 8:278); Gregory of Nyssa, *That There Are Not Three Gods* (*NPNF²* 5:331–36).

41. Athanasius, *Letter to Serapion*.

42. Gregory of Nazianzus, *Oration 31* (*NPNF²* 7:318f.).

43. Kelly, *Early Christian Creeds*, 297–98.

44. *NPNF²* 5:334.

Chapter 3

1. A short survey of the events in this controversy can be found in Richard A. Norris Jr., *The Christological Controversy* (Philadel-

phia: Fortress, 1980). The standard work dealing with the theological positions is still R. V. Sellers, *Two Ancient Christologies* (London: SPCK, 1954). Translations of selections from important documents are found in Norris and in J. Stevenson, *Creeds, Councils and Controversies: Documents Illustrative of the History of the Church A.D. 337–461* (New York: Seabury Press, 1966). An informative, helpful, and controversial study of this controversy is found in Donald Fairbairn, *Grace and Christology in the Early Church* (Oxford: Oxford University Press, 2003). Fairbain challenges the belief that the positions of Alexandria and Antioch can be neatly divided into distinct "schools."

2. Apollinaris, *Fragments*, 45, 72; in Norris, *Christological Controversy*, 109.

3. Apollinaris, *Fragments*, 89; in Norris, *Christological Controversy*, 110.

4. Gregory of Nazianzus, *Ep.* 101. 7 (*NPNF²* 7:440). See Brian E. Daley, " 'Heavenly man' and 'Eternal Christ': Apollinaris and Gregory of Nyssa on the Personal Identity of the Savior," *Journal of Early Christian Studies* (Winter 2002): 468–88.

5. Theodore of Mopsuestia, *On the Incarnation*, especially Books V, VII, VIII, XII in Norris, *Christological Controversy*, 113f.

6. Nestorius, *First Sermon against the Theotokos*, in Norris, *Christological Controversy*, 123f.

7. Fairbairn, *Grace and Christology*, 40f.

8. Cyril, *Twelve Anathemas against Nestorius* (*NPNF²* 3:25).

9. Theodoret, *Response to Cyril* (*NPNF²* 3:26f.).

10. Cyril, *Letter to John of Antioch* (*NPNF²* 14:251–53).

11. Leo I, *Letter to Flavian* (Letter 28). It is commonly known as the *Tome*, as indicated in the text (*NPNF²* 12:38–43; 14:254–58). A great deal of the theology behind this document came from John Cassian; see Fairbairn, *Grace and Christology*, 133–99. Of course, the hand of Augustine is also evident.

12. *NPNF²* 12:71.

13. *NPNF²* 14:264–65.

14. See Robert Louis Wilken, *The Spirit of Early Christian Thought* (New Haven: Yale University Press, 2003), 133–35.

15. John of Damascus, *On the Divine Images*, trans. David Anderson (Crestwood, New York: St. Vladimir's Seminary Press, 1980), I.5–19, p. 16–27.

Chapter 4

1. The standard biography of Augustine is the highly detailed work by Peter Brown, *Augustine of Hippo: A Biography* (Berkeley: University of California Press, 1967).

2. Augustine, *Confessions,* III.1.1 (*NPNF*[1] 1:60).

3. Augustine, *Confessions,* VII.9f. (*NPNF*[1] 1:108).

4. Augustine, *The Happy Life,* pref.

5. Augustine, *Confessions,* VIII.6–12 (*NPNF*[1] 1:121–28).

6. Augustine, *Confessions,* I.1 (*NPNF*[1] 1:45).

7. Augustine, Letter XIII.2 (*NPNF*[1] 1:230–31); Augustine, *On Music,* VI.4–5, 7, 9, 13.

8. Augustine, *On the Morals of the Catholic Church,* 5.7–6.9 (*NPNF*[1] 4:43–44).

9. Augustine, *On Free Will,* I.21, 26, 29 (LCC 6:125, 127–30).

10. Augustine, *On Christian Doctrine,* I.11.11 (*NPNF*[1] 2:525); Augustine, *On Free Will,* III.10.30 (LCC 6:189–90).

11. Augustine, *Exposition on Eighty-Four Propositions in the Epistle to the Romans,* 4(4), 4,5; 34, 41.

12. Augustine, *To Simplician, on Diverse Questions,* I.2.2, 2.3, 2.7, 2.12, 2.13, 2.21 (LCC 6:386–88, 391, 394–95, 404–05). See also Augustine, *On the Spirit and the Letter,* 5 (*NPNF*[1] 5:84–85).

13. The standard work on Pelagius is the classic by Georges de Plinval, *Pelage: se secrits, sa vie, et sa reforme* (Lausanne: Libraire Payot, 1943).

14. The references to Pelagius's work are taken from his *Letter to Demetrias.*

15. *NPNF*[1] 1:33.

16. Augustine, *On the Good of Perseverence,* 53 (*NPNF*[1] 5:xv, 547).

17. Augustine, *On the Proceedings of Pelagius,* 24 (*NPNF*[1] 5:193–94).

18. Augustine, *On Merits and on the Remission of Sins, and on the Baptism of Infants,* I.10, 11, 19 (*NPNF*[1] 5:18–19, 22).

19. Augustine, *On Merits,* II.27 (*NPNF*[1] 5:55–56); Augustine, *On Original Sin,* 39 (*NPNF*[1] 5:251).

20. Augustine, *On Nature and Grace,* 3 (*NPNF*[1] 5:122).

21. Augustine, *On the Spirit and the Letter,* 47 (*NPNF*[1] 5:103).

22. Augustine, *On Nature and Grace,* 25 (*NPNF*[1] 5:129–130).

23. Augustine, *The Spirit and the Letter,* 5 (*NPNF*[1] 5:84–85).

24. Augustine, *On the Proceedings of Pelagius*, 33, 34 (*NPNF*[1] 5:198–199); Augustine, *On the Spirit and the Letter*, 53, 54, 56, 60 (*NPNF*[1] 5:106–108, 110).

25. Augustine, *On the Spirit and the Letter*, 8 (*NPNF*[1] 5:86).

26. Augustine, *On Merits*, II.8 (*NPNF*[1] 5:47); Augustine, *On Man's Perfection in Righteousness*, 10f. (*NPNF*[1] 5:162); Augustine, *On the Proceedings of Pelagius*, 20 (*NPNF*[1] 5:191–192).

27. Augustine, *On Merits*, I.70; II.4 (*NPNF*[1] 5:43, 45); Augustine, *On Nature and Grace*, 51, 53 (*NPNF*[1] 5:138–139).

28. Augustine, *On Original Sin*, 28 (*NPNF*[1] 5:84–85); Augustine, *On the Proceedings of Pelagius*, 35 (*NPNF*[1] 5:84–85).

29. Augustine, *Against the Two Letters of the Pelagians*, II.2, 3; III.25 (*NPNF*[1] 5:392, 414–415).

30. Augustine, *On Grace and Free Will*, 2–4, 11.

31. Augustine, *On Grace and Free Will*, 13, 25, 27, 31, 33; Augustine, *On Predestination*, 30, 43 (*NPNF*[1] 5:536–537, 543); Augustine, *On Rebuke and Grace*, 17 (*NPNF*[1] 5:478).

32. Augustine, *On the Gift of Perseverance*, 25, 37, 41 (*NPNF*[1] 5:534–535, 539); Augustine, *On Rebuke and Grace*, 12, 45 (*NPNF*[1] 5:476, 489); Augustine, *On Predestination*, 15, 16 (*NPNF*[1] 5:505–506).

33. Augustine, *On Predestination*, 19, 30 (*NPNF*[1] 5:507–508, 512); Augustine, *On Rebuke and Grace*, 30 (*NPNF*[1] 5:483–484); Augustine, *On the Gift of Perseverance*, 67 (*NPNF*[1] 5:552).

34. Augustine, *On Rebuke and Grace*, 25 (*NPNF*[1] 5:482); Augustine, *On Predestination*, 13 (*NPNF*[1] 5:504–505).

35. Donald Fairbairn, *Grace and Christology in the Early Church* (Oxford: Oxford University Press, 2003), 12.

36. See, for example, Augustine, *On Merits*, I.10, 39, 60; III.8 (*NPNF*[1] 5:18–19, 30, 38–39).

37. Augustine, *Sermon 162*.

38. Augustine, *On Original Sin*, 46 (*NPNF*[1] 5:253); Augustine, *Ennarations on the Psalms* 33, 4–5 (*NPNF*[1] 8:71).

39. Augustine, *On Original Sin*, 45, 46 (*NPNF*[1] 5:252–253); Augustine, *On Merits*, I.61, 63 (*NPNF*[1] 5:39–40).

40. Augustine, *Against the Two Letters of the Pelagians*, II.21 (*NPNF*[1] 5:400–401).

41. Augustine, *On Predestination*, 7 (*NPNF*[1] 5:500–501).

The Three Universal or Ecumenical Creeds

The Apostles' Creed

I believe in God, the Father Almighty, maker of heaven and earth.

And in Jesus Christ, His only Son, our Lord, who was conceived by the Holy Spirit, born of the virgin Mary, suffered under Pontius Pilate, was crucified, died and was buried. He descended into hell. The third day He rose again from the dead. He ascended into heaven and sits at the right hand of God the Father Almighty. From thence He will come to judge the living and the dead.

I believe in the Holy Spirit, the holy Christian Church, the communion of saints, the forgiveness of sins, the resurrection of the body, and the life everlasting. Amen.

The Nicene Creed

I believe in one God, the Father Almighty, maker of heaven and earth and of all things visible and invisible.

And in one Lord Jesus Christ, the only-begotten Son of God, begotten of His Father before all worlds, God of God, Light of Light, very God of very God, begotten, not made, being of one substance with the Father, by whom all things were made; who for us men and for our salvation came down from heaven and was incarnate by the Holy Spirit of the virgin Mary and was made man; and was crucified also for us under Pontius Pilate. He suffered and was buried. And the third day He rose again according to the Scriptures and ascended into heaven and sits at the right hand of the Father. And He will come again with glory to judge both the living and the dead, whose kingdom will have no end.

And I believe in the Holy Spirit, the Lord and Giver of Life, who proceeds from the Father and the Son, who with the Father and the Son together is worshiped and glorified, who spoke by the prophets. And I believe in one holy Christian and apostolic Church, I acknowledge one Baptism for the remission of sins, and I look for the resurrection of the dead and the life of the world to come. Amen.

The Creed of Athanasius

Written against the Arians.

Whoever desires to be saved must, above all, hold the catholic faith.

Whoever does not keep it whole and undefiled will without doubt perish eternally.

And the catholic faith is this,

that we worship one God in trinity and Trinity in unity, neither confusing the persons nor dividing the substance.

For the Father is one person, the Son is another, and the Holy Spirit is another.

But the Godhead of the Father and of the Son and of the Holy Spirit is one: the glory equal, the majesty coeternal.

Such as the Father is, such is the Son, and such is the Holy Spirit:

the Father uncreated, the Son uncreated, the Holy Spirit uncreated;

the Father infinite, the Son infinite, the Holy Spirit infinite;

the Father eternal, the Son eternal, the Holy Spirit eternal.

And yet there are not three Eternals, but one Eternal,

just as there are not three Uncreated or three Infinites, but one Uncreated and one Infinite.

In the same way, the Father is almighty, the Son almighty, the Holy Spirit almighty;

and yet there are not three Almighties but one Almighty.

So the Father is God, the Son is God, the Holy Spirit is God;

and yet there are not three Gods, but one God.

So the Father is Lord, the Son is Lord, the Holy Spirit is Lord;

and yet there are not three Lords, but one Lord.

Just as we are compelled by the Christian truth to acknowledge each distinct person as God and Lord,

so also are we prohibited by the catholic religion to say that there are three Gods or Lords.

The Father is not made nor created nor begotten by anyone.

The Son is neither made nor created, but begotten of the Father alone.

The Holy Spirit is of the Father and of the Son, neither made nor created nor begotten but proceeding.

Thus, there is one Father, not three Fathers; one Son, not three Sons; one Holy Spirit, not three Holy Spirits.

And in this Trinity none is before or after another; none is greater or less than another;

but the whole three persons are coeternal with each other and coequal so that in all things, as has been stated above, the Trinity in Unity and Unity in Trinity is to be worshiped.

Therefore, whoever desires to be saved must think thus about the Trinity.

But it is also necessary for everlasting salvation that one faithfully believe the incarnation of our Lord Jesus Christ.

Therefore, it is the right faith that we believe and confess that our Lord Jesus Christ, the Son of God, is at the same time both God and man.

He is God, begotten from the substance of the Father before all ages; and He is man, born from the substance of His mother in this age:

perfect God and perfect man, composed of a rational soul and human flesh;

equal to the Father with respect to His divinity, less than the Father with respect to His humanity.

Although He is God and man, He is not two, but one Christ:

one, however, not by the conversion of the divinity into flesh but by the assumption of the humanity into God;

one altogether, not by confusion of substance, but by unity of person.

For as the rational soul and flesh is one man, so God and man is one Christ,

who suffered for our salvation, descended into hell, rose again on the third day from the dead,

ascended into heaven, and is seated at the right hand of the Father, from whence He will come to judge the living and the dead.

At His coming all people will rise again with their bodies and give an account concerning their own deeds.

And those who have done good will enter into eternal life, and those who have done evil into eternal fire.

This is the catholic faith; whoever does not believe it faithfully and firmly cannot be saved.